Online Research Methods for Psychologists

Online Research Methods for Psychologists

Neil Coulson

University of Nottingham, UK

First published 2015 by
PALGRAVE

Palgrave in the UK is an imprint of Macmillan Publishers Limited, registered in England, company number 785998, of 4 Crinan Street, London, N1 9XW.

Palgrave Macmillan in the US is a division of St Martin's Press LLC, 175 Fifth Avenue, New York, NY 10010.

Palgrave is a global imprint of the above companies and is represented throughout the world.

Palgrave® and Macmillan® are registered trademarks in the United States, the United Kingdom, Europe and other countries.

ISBN 978–1–137–00575–5

This book is printed on paper suitable for recycling and made from fully managed and sustained forest sources. Logging, pulping and manufacturing processes are expected to conform to the environmental regulations of the country of origin.

A catalogue record for this book is available from the British Library.

A catalog record for this book is available from the Library of Congress.

Typeset by MPS Limited, Chennai, India.

Printed in China

This book is dedicated to the memory of my much loved grandparents, Mary and Alan Cadman, whose support throughout the years as I was growing up will never be forgotten. Without them I would never have been able to pursue my interest in Psychology at University and embark on an academic career. You are both much loved and terribly missed.

Contents

List of Tables   viii

List of Boxes   ix

Preface   x

Acknowledgements   xii

1   Introduction to Online Research   1

2   Online Interviews   33

3   Online Focus Groups   51

4   Online Surveys   81

5   Online Experiments   112

6   Social Media as a Research Environment   119

Appendix A: Participant Information Page – Online Survey Example   150

Appendix B: Consent – Online Survey Example   153

Appendix C: Debrief and Thank You   154

Glossary   155

References   159

Index   170

List of Tables

3.1   Example structure of online discussion forum   66
3.2   Commonly used abbreviations in online
      communication   74
3.3   Selected chat and forum software packages   79
4.1   Selected online survey software packages   109
6.1   An illustration of Kaplan & Haenlein's (2010)
      classification of social media   121
6.2   Selected software packages   148

List of Boxes

1.1	Access to the Internet and engagement with social networking	4
1.2	Example of research about the Internet using the Internet	15
1.3	Ethical principles for conducting research with human participants	21
2.1	Example of asynchronous online interviews using email	39
2.2	Example of synchronous online interview using instant messaging	46
2.3	Developing online interview questions	49
3.1	Example of asynchronous online focus group	56
3.2	Strategies for encouraging participation in asynchronous online focus groups	61
3.3	Example of synchronous online focus group using a chat room	69
3.4	Using Skype for focus group research	72
4.1	Online survey response option formats	84
4.2	Probability sampling procedures for closed populations	93
5.1	Online psychological research websites	114
6.1	Why do people blog?	124
6.2	Example of analysis of Twitter	126
6.3	Social network sites: a brief history	129
6.4	Example of text-reduction analysis of online forums	139
6.5	Example of in-depth analysis of online forum	141
6.6	Examples of YouTube as a research environment	144

Preface

Online Research Methods for Psychologists is a textbook designed for those who are both new to psychological research being undertaken through the Internet as well as for those who have some experience but who wish to further develop their online methodological expertise and skills. In writing this textbook, an assumption is made as to the areas of potential interest that readers may have. That is to say, readers may be interested in how the Internet may be useful in the collection of data that has typically been undertaken via offline 'traditional' methods, such as a face-to-face interview or self-administered paper and pencil survey. Alternatively, readers may be interested in researching aspects of online behaviour, such as social networking or participation in online discussion forums. Regardless of the reason for exploring the role of the Internet as a tool to undertake psychological research, it is fair to say that with increasing access to the Internet and significant advances in functionality, there has never been a more exciting time in which to explore and use online research methods.

This textbook is organized in a series of chapters reflecting specific methodologies. It begins with Chapter 1, which discusses the background and history of the Internet and considers some of the basic advantages and disadvantages of using online methods in psychological research as well as key ethical issues that researchers should consider when designing and running their online studies. In Chapter 2, the online interview is the focus of discussion, with the email interview and those undertaken through instant messaging being considered. In Chapter 3, we discuss both asynchronous and synchronous online focus groups and consider the relative strengths and weaknesses of both these main types together with some practical tips on how best to engage with them. Chapter 4 discusses what is probably the most popular online tool used by psychologists, namely the online survey, and provides the reader with a useful overview of the key issues to consider including design, recruitment and response rate as well as issues surrounding bias and sampling. In Chapter 5, we consider the role of online experiments in psychological research. The textbook concludes with Chapter 6 where we explore social media as a research environment and look at some specific examples, such as blogs, forums and social networking sites and consider the possibilities that such novel online examples of social media offer to psychologists.

In order to assist the reader, this textbook includes a number of useful features. For example, throughout the chapters there are some examples of past psychological research that have employed online methods, and reflections from those investigators are captured and presented. In addition, some suggested online software packages are included together with some brief information concerning the important issue of cost. There is a glossary at the end of the textbook and some suggested reading is proposed at the end of each chapter that can be followed up at the reader's convenience.

And finally...

The Internet is a fascinating beast and can be used for many diverse purposes. Undertaking psychological research is only one of them. As we go forward, we will undoubtedly learn more about our efforts to harness the potential of online methods in research and so this textbook represents a timely summary of where we are now in this journey.

Acknowledgements

I would like to express my gratitude to Paul from Palgrave for having the vision to see the potential of this book and to Isabel for guiding me through the process. I would also like to thank the anonymous reviewers both at the proposal stage as well as the end product.

CHAPTER 1

Introduction to Online Research

This chapter begins with a brief historical overview of the development of the Internet and how it has evolved since it was first conceived. From this we will consider how the Internet may be a useful tool through which to engage in psychological research. A range of examples will be provided that describe three broad types of psychological research that has been undertaken in recent years: translational, phenomenological and novel research. Having been introduced to some brief examples, a range of potential benefits that may arise from using the Internet for psychological research will be explored as well as potential challenges or difficulties that may be encountered. Next, we consider the ethical implications of using the Internet as a research tool and reflect on a number of important ethical principles that should be considered when using online methods. In doing so, attention will be given to the important guidance published by the British Psychological Society (2013) and the main issues raised in this guidance will be outlined and discussed. Finally, we consider some practical advice on how to behave and conduct oneself online.

The Internet: background, history and development

The origins of the Internet are located in the Advanced Research Projects Agency Network (ARPANET) which was initially funded by the Advanced Research Projects Agency (ARPA) within the US Department of Defense for use by its projects at universities and laboratories across the US. The first four nodes on this network were added in 1969 and were the University of California, Los Angeles, the Stanford Research Institute, the University of California Santa Barbara and the University of Utah. By 1971 a total of 15 nodes had been added, and in that year email was also invented by Ray Tomlinson of BBN (Bolt Beranek and Newman, Inc) and included within the ARPANET in 1972. In 1973, the first international connections were made by adding nodes in England (University College London) and Norway (NORSAR). The first commercial version of ARPANET was launched by BBN in 1974 and was called TELENET. From this point onwards a number of network systems were developed, including USENET in 1979 and BITNET in 1981. In 1982, the Defense Communications Agency (DCA) established the Transmission Control Protocol (TCP) and Internet Protocol (IP), as the protocol suite, commonly known as TCP/IP. The Internet, as we know it, in essence began with this standardization and represents networked TCP/IP systems. Today, the Internet is a global system of interconnected computer networks that uses the standard IP suite (TCP/IP) to serve billions of users worldwide.

By early 1995 a number of changes had taken place with computer and Internet technology that made the Internet more suited to carrying out psychological research. Improvements in hardware and software made computers less expensive to buy and easier to use, there were exponential increases in the number of people with Internet access. Web browsers became more sophisticated and were better at handling complex multimedia content, and Hypertext Markup Language (HTML) 2 made it possible for web pages to display forms where participants can answer questions and submit their responses for storage on a remote server (Birnbaum, 2004). This made the Internet an important research tool that is qualitatively different to other forms of electronic connectivity like the television, radio or telephone (Hewson, Laurent, & Vogel, 1996). The Internet combines the wide reach of mass broadcast technologies like radio and television with a level of interactivity that allows individuals to interact almost instantaneously with other people who could be located anywhere in the world (Bargh & McKenna, 2004).

The Internet as a research tool

The Internet has arguably had a profound impact on how we live our lives and has touched almost every aspect of daily life. For example, we can book an airline ticket, download music, find lost friends and family or do an online degree. Similarly, the Internet has created many new opportunities to undertake psychological research and throughout this textbook we shall be exploring some of the more popular ways through which the Internet can be used. Indeed, over the last 10–15 years we have accrued much experience in using the Internet for research purposes and have learnt from the successes and failures of other researchers.

Perhaps the starting point for our review of potential online methods that may be useful for psychological research is in fact an acknowledgement that the people we are interested in studying and working with have access to the Internet. This may seem an odd point to make but consider the situation 20 years ago, would such a textbook be needed or indeed relevant? Rather, it is fair to say that over the past couple of decades or so access to the Internet has grown exponentially and more recently we have also seen a rise in social networking sites, such as Facebook. Indeed, at the time of writing this textbook Facebook celebrated its 10th anniversary. From a research perspective, the issue is whether sufficient numbers of people have access to the Internet or engage in social networking to render any samples we may generate as free from bias or not. That is to say, if we were to sample Internet users, would they represent the wider population or be biased in some way? This issue has been fiercely debated over the years but as the number of people with access to the Internet continues to increase this issue may become less relevant. However, it is an issue worth bearing in mind as we begin our journey through *Online Research Methods for Psychologists* (see Box 1.1, Access to the Internet and engagement with social networking).[1]

As we might imagine, the Internet has been used widely in psychological research. In a review of research published by the American Psychological Association (during 2003–2004) as well as additional studies that used the Internet to collect data ($N = 121$), Skitka & Sargis (2006) identified and described three approaches to conducting psychological research using the Internet. Let us take a look at each of these in turn to better understand how the Internet has made an impact on psychological research.

---

1 Readers interested in obtaining reasonably up to date UK, European and worldwide facts and figures about access to the Internet and engagement in social networking through use of Facebook should consult: www.internetworldstats.com.

BOX 1.1 Access to the Internet and engagement with social networking

According to the Office for National Statistics (2014), approximately 92% of the adult UK population had used the Internet. This represents 59 million people and when asked, 76% of the adult UK population said they used the Internet every day and this is an increase of 21 million from 2006 (when comparable records began). Similarly, accessing the Internet from a mobile phone also increased from 24% in 2010 to 58% in 2014. Approximately 22 million households (84%) had Internet access, which has risen from 57% in 2006.

While Internet use has always tended to be higher in younger age groups, there has been a sizeable increase in the number of 65+ who report using a computer every day. For example, in 2006 only 9% reported using one every day compared with 42% in 2014. In 2013, adults aged 16–24 years were the most likely to use the Internet for leisure or recreation, particularly social networking (91%), reading or downloading online news (65%), Internet banking (56%) or using services related to travel or travel accommodation (38%).

Social networking has proven to be a popular activity with approximately 54% of adults in the UK engaging in this online activity in 2014. While social networking is most popular among the young (see previous paragraph), it has also become popular among older groups with one in every two adults (54%) aged 45–54 years old indicating that they engage in social networking.

Accessing the Internet via other mobile devices, such as laptops or tablets, appears to be popular with approximately 58% of UK adults reporting doing so. The age group most likely to do so is the 25–34 year olds with 86% accessing the Internet 'on the go'. In the 65+ the figure is approximately 1 in 10 (11%) who access the Internet in such a way.

Translational approach

First of all, 59% of research studies employed a translational approach in which methods and/or materials that were originally developed for offline use were adapted for use on the Internet. A common example of this is taking traditional paper and pencil questionnaires and converting them into a web format. For example,

Srivastava *et al.* (2003) were interested in nature versus nurture models of personality development and translated the Big Five personality inventory to a web-based version to test different predictions from biological and contextualist theories of personality (i.e. the biological model predicts that personality should be relatively stable by adulthood, whereas the contextualist model posits that people's personality is affected by changes in their life circumstances over time, therefore we should witness considerable variability in personality types across different age cohorts). A total of 132,515 adults aged from 21 to 60 completed their online personality inventory and the results revealed much variability in the distributions of the Big Five across different age cohorts, including those older than 30 and so they argued that their cross-sectional data were better explained by the contextualist account of personality development.

Other examples include studies that have modified Milgram's (1977) 'lost-letter' technique to study attitudes online by sending 'lost' email messages to naive study participants. For example, Vaes *et al.* (2003) examined whether participants would be more likely to reply to a 'lost' email message as a function of whether the message sender was a member of an in- or out-group, and whether the sender's message expressed a primary or secondary emotion. The participants were 400 academics at a Belgian university who received an email from the researchers. The first line of the email included an expression of primary (e.g. 'I'm beside myself with rage') or secondary emotion ('I'm filled with indignation') and group membership was manipulated by having the email from a researcher at the same or a different university. The researchers examined whether the email was forwarded on to the intended recipient and also coded the explanatory note that tended to accompany the email. While the researchers found no differences of emotion or group membership on overall forwarding rates of the 'lost' emails, they did find that forwarded messages expressed higher levels of solidarity with the original message sender if it came from an in-group member who expressed a secondary emotion.

Phenomenological approach

Second, 36% of studies employed a phenomenological approach where online behaviour is the phenomenon of interest to the researcher. That is to say, they are interested in how the use of the Internet as well as Internet-based interaction may influence people's thoughts, feelings and behaviour. This type of research, for example, has focussed on the use of online communities, blogs and social networking and exploring the relationship between Internet use and well-being.

The work of McKenna and colleagues illustrates nicely the potential research opportunities arising from online communities. In their work, they have explored the potential of the Internet to allow people to experiment with new or less well-accepted aspects of their identities. For example, McKenna & Bargh (1998) contacted samples of individuals who had frequently posted comments to online community forums for those with stigmatized sexual identities (e.g. alt.homosexual, alt.bondage; Study 2) or political ideologies (e.g. alt.skinheads, misc.activism.milita; Study 3). They also tried to recruit those who lurked online but did not contribute by posting messages to encourage participation in the study. The research team found some evidence in support of the notion that participation in these online communities led to important interpersonal and psychological consequences for those involved. In particular, individuals who explored alternative identities in online communities considered their marginal identity as increasingly important, and this sense of importance was linked to higher levels of self-acceptance and to disclosing the marginalized identity to friends and family.

Other examples cited by Skitka & Sargis (2006) include a study by Blanchard (2004) who examined the sense of community among those individuals who either participated in or followed the Julie/Julia blog. Julie, a web blogger, systematically worked her way through each and every recipe in Julia Child's *Mastering the Art of French Cooking* book over the course of about a year and wrote about her experiences online. Each day the blog received thousands of hits and provided a forum through which blog readers could comment and others (or the author) could respond. Blanchard was able to obtain permission to post a link on the site that directed blog readers to an online survey that examined reactions to the blog. Blanchard found in the results that reading blogs did create a modest sense of community, and active participation through posting comments was associated with a stronger sense of community with other blog participants.

In terms of Internet use and well-being, Kraut and colleagues were interested in how use of the Internet impacts upon and tested two hypotheses about this relationship. One hypothesis suggests that because the Internet can actually facilitate social interaction (e.g. email, instant messaging) time spent online should be related to greater social connections and as a result will facilitate psychological well-being. The alternative hypothesis argues the opposite that as time available for face-to-face interaction decreases, this will be related to greater social isolation and therefore poorer psychological well-being. In order to examine these hypotheses, Kraut *et al.* (1998) examined the Internet use behaviours of 93 households (i.e. server logs of hours spent online, email volume, number of websites visited per week) and found that as time spent on the Internet increased, involvement in real world social interaction decreased. Those participants who spent more time online also tended to report higher levels of loneliness and depression, relative to before they first obtained access to the Internet.

In a follow up study by Kraut *et al.*, (2002) with the same participants two years later, they found that they had in fact adapted to having Internet access at home. These findings reported no association between the hours spent online and reported loneliness and that depression was in fact lower among the heaviest users of the Internet. The authors suggested that although there may be short-term negative consequences, after a while, increased use of the Internet is in fact associated with greater social support and higher levels of well-being.

Novel approach

Finally, 5% of research studies employed a novel approach with methodologies that are unique to online research and not seen in non-Internet based research and were noted by the review authors for their creativity. In particular, a number of examples were highlighted that the authors felt captured the truly new innovative ways in which the Internet was creating new opportunities for research. Let us have a look at a couple of the examples mentioned.

In a study by Rentfrow & Gosling (2003, Study 4), information that was freely available on the Internet was used to examine specific hypotheses concerning the psychology of music preferences. In their study, the music libraries of 500 individuals from the USA, which were available from websites dedicated to music sharing and downloading, were examined. The study authors categorized their music preferences according to genre. The aim of this study was to explore whether the dimensionality in music preferences evidenced through music libraries was consistent with those found when people were asked to report directly their music tastes and preferences (Rentfrow & Gosling, Study 2). In their results, it was revealed that there did exist a considerable convergence across the different means of assessing and describing music preferences.

In another example, Shobat & Musch (2003) were interested in exploring whether there existed any ethnic discrimination on a German auction website. In order to do this they planted vendors of similar products but varied the ethnicity of their surnames. The results revealed that vendors with a Turkish surname (a minority group in Germany) took longer to receive winning bids than those with German names.

Methodological observations

As well as reviewing and describing the types of research questions evident within the sample of online research studies, Skitka & Sargis (2006) also considered the methodological characteristics of the psychological research that had taken place online.

Their analysis found that the majority of studies (54%) used an experimental methodology. That is to say, the research deliberately and explicitly included the manipulation of at least one variable. They noted that several of these studies randomly assigned participants to different forms, using HTML code. Of the remaining studies, 39% employed a correlational design, 4% were qualitative and 3% were descriptive.

Skitka & Sargis (2006) also noted the various types of samples used by researchers in their review of online research. They reported that 25% of the studies used online research methods to collect data from college students, 36% targeted specific groups of participants, 35% used opt-in samples. A further 1% used a random sample (i.e. studies that adopted this approach subcontracted their research to a company that had created a nationally representative panel of web-enabled households). The remaining 1% did not report any details of how they obtained their sample.

From this brief summary, we can see the types of psychological research studies that have been undertaken and that have used online methods. In the following section, we will consider some of the potential benefits that may arise when using online methods to undertake psychological research.

Potential benefits of online data collection

There are many potential advantages to conducting research on the Internet. Indeed, as our experiences have grown with regards psychological research conducted online, so too do our insights into the ways in which this research medium may differ from traditional methods, for example, face-to-face interviews or paper and pencil surveys. It is fair to say that many of the advantages evident in online research are related to issues of access, cost and overall efficiency. However, researchers should not forget that the Internet might also provide new opportunities for research as well as allow new approaches to the study of complex behaviours or those where traditional methods may be less effective. In this section a number of these potential benefits will be summarized but many of them will be revisited and discussed in later chapters when specific online methods are considered.

Access to participants

Traditional methods of recruitment often involve cooperating with a 'gatekeeper' to gain access to participants in a particular organization or clinical setting. The level of cooperation with staff at these institutions can influence the outcome and success of the study. Online recruitment can minimize these difficulties by allowing researchers to gain direct access to participants without going through a 'gatekeeper', although permission may still be needed from the moderators of a website before posting an announcement about a study and inviting people to take part (Hamilton & Bowers, 2006). We shall consider recruitment in more detail later on in the textbook (see Chapter 4 – Online Surveys).

Hard-to-reach populations

The growing number of people who use the Internet means that researchers have the potential to recruit participants from a more varied range of backgrounds and geographical areas than would otherwise be possible. Online recruitment allows researchers to target specific sample groups (Hewson *et al.*, 1996) and recruit participants with characteristics that arise infrequently among the general population (Birnbaum, 2004). For example, the Internet can be used to study individuals who might otherwise be difficult to contact, such as those who suffer from a rare illness (Hennekam, 2011) or who fall outside the health care system because they have not sought professional help for a problem that they suffer from (Granello & Wheaton, 2004). Several techniques can be used to recruit participants on the Internet, including passively letting people find the study using an Internet search engine, emailing prospective participants, contacting related organizations and asking them to promote the study in their newsletter, posting information about the study in online communities and placing adverts on other websites (Birnbaum, 2004).

Reduced costs

Undertaking psychological research using the Internet may be cheaper compared with other methods of data collection (Hewson *et al.*, 1996). For example, if a survey is being undertaken online then there are no costs attached to buying stationary or printing copies of the survey (see Chapter 4 for further discussion of online surveys). Similarly, if an email interview study is being conducted then there are no costs arising from the purchase of a Dictaphone. Furthermore, there are no costs attached to the purchase of a transcription unit or any costs of paying someone to transcribe each interview (see Chapter 2 for further discussion of online interviews). For many online studies it is possible to design the research so that the data generated can be downloaded and automatically imported into the analysis software (e.g. SPSS or NVivo), avoiding the time and expense associated with entering data manually. However, there can be hidden costs involved with programming an online experiment and obtaining the server space to host it, and if a technical 'help desk' is provided to assist participants with any problems they might encounter while taking part in a study then this can drastically increase the costs involved in administering an online experiment (Granello & Wheaton, 2004). Overall, though, it is widely regarded that online psychological research can bring with it financial savings and efficiencies which may be helpful to those researchers with limited or no funds (e.g. student projects).

Researcher anonymity & demand characteristics

Online studies help the researcher to remain anonymous, which can potentially reduce demand characteristics (Hewson *et al.*, 1996). Demand characteristics arise when participants behave differently to how they would normally, for example, because of wanting to please the researcher or trying to support the experimental hypothesis (Nichols & Maner, 2008; Orne, 1962). The anonymity conferred through the Internet may also help to reduce or eliminate researcher bias. Research bias is where the researcher behaves differently depending on personal characteristics like the age, gender or ethnicity of the study participant (Hewson *et al.*, 1996). However, the anonymity conferred online may also have negative consequences as it may limit the extent to which rapport between the researcher and the study participant becomes sufficiently well developed, and the consequences of this are less clear (Benfield & Szlemko, 2006). Later in this chapter (Section 1.5 'Potential challenges of online data collection'), the issue of anonymity is returned to and further discussed.

Flexibility and convenience

Researchers undertaking studies online may find that it is considered more flexible by participants and that they appreciate being able to take part in research studies at their convenience and in their own time. For example, when using traditional methods of data collection like face-to-face focus groups or telephone interviews, participants are likely to have to travel to a specific venue or tailor their schedule to fit in with the times when the researcher is available, which might not always be convenient (Hewson *et al.*, 1996). With online psychological research studies, data collection can take place 24 hours a day, 7 days a week for as long as is required (Birnbaum, 2004). Moreover, the amount of time needed for online data collection can also be independent of the sample size required because many people can take part at the same time, as is the case for an online interview or online survey (Skitka & Sargis, 2006). Indeed, it has been argued that response times can be quicker when collecting data online (Granello & Wheaton, 2004), allowing researchers to collect data in days or weeks rather than months (Skitka & Sargis, 2006). In later chapters we shall discuss specific online methods and explore how they may be helpful to researcher and participant alike.

Observing social behaviour

Psychologists interested in various aspects of social behaviour now have new opportunities and resources available as a result of the Internet. For example, there are now many more opportunities to access archives of communication across a wide variety of topic domains (e.g. hobbies, lifestyle, popular culture, illness). Indeed, psychologists have been able to undertake research exploring a range of social processes, such as self-help mechanisms (Malik & Coulson, 2010a, 2011), negotiation (Biesenbach-Lucas & Weasen-forth, 2002) and identity formation (McKenna & Bargh, 1998) to name but a few.

Kraut *et al.*, (2002) argue that as a result of the many online forums available to researchers, the study of a range of phenomena is now much easier in comparison to traditional methods. For example, the development and evolution of groups or learning over time may be particularly difficult to research as a result of the challenges associated with bringing study participants to the research laboratory on several occasions. Indeed, many researchers argue that the Internet has provided a new means through which to study large group behaviour over a period of time. For example, Butler (2001) was able to study the impact of participation on the attraction and retention of group members, by creating an archive of all messages sent to 206 online groups over a 3-month period.

Furthermore, in contrast to traditional observational research that is conducted in a face-to-face context, such as in a classroom or playground, where the researcher's presence may contaminate the phenomenon under study, researchers can be less obtrusive when undertaking observation online. For example, Bruckman (1999) examined the influence of groups on long-term learning, by tracking 475 children learning a programming language over a 5-year period. In addition, because the study participants were able to type their own comments there was no need for transcription and through simple content analysis packages, the researcher was able to examine age-related and gender differences in how the children engaged with the learning tool.

Access to other archival data

The Internet has also allowed researchers the opportunity to access detailed and more importantly unobtrusive data concerning a range of phenomena besides social behaviour. For example, the detailed activity logs generated by Internet users across a range of online activities (e.g. browsing behaviour, purchase behaviour, email sending, social networking behaviour) can yield a valuable source of data for psychologists.

Stigmatized identities

The Internet can also be a valuable tool for studying groups that have a stigmatized identity. Stigmas vary on dimensions such as visibility, severity or social disruptiveness, and individuals can be stigmatized on a range of characteristics including skin colour, facial deformity, physical disability, obesity, sexual orientation and mental illness (Crocker & Major, 1989). Some health conditions like cancer, AIDS and alcoholism may also carry a negative social stigma because of misconceptions about the causes of these diseases or due to moral issues associated with them, like the idea that alcoholics lack control over their drinking behaviour (Wright & Bell, 2003). Individuals with stigmatized identities may find it easier to discuss problems and seek social support by taking part in online support communities rather than attending face-to-face support groups (White & Dorman, 2001), and there is tentative evidence that members of stigmatized groups are more supportive of taking part in studies that use online surveys (see Chapter 4) instead of being asked to complete paper and pencil surveys (Trau et al., 2013).

New social phenomena

While much of the preceding comments have discussed how the Internet has offered greater flexibility, access, convenience and efficiency with regards conducting research, we must not lose sight of the fact that the Internet is indeed a phenomenon in itself and therefore may be the subject of psychological research. Indeed, there has been a growing body of literature that describes research studies undertaken to examine many diverse aspects of Internet use and issues raised by online behaviour (e.g. social networking, online self-help, relationship formation, trust and deception). As a result, many researchers nowadays are conducting research *about* the Internet *using* the Internet (see Box 1.2) and further examples of this can be found throughout later chapters.

In summary, researchers may find there is a range of potentially helpful benefits arising from the use of online methods to conduct psychological research. In later chapters, some of these benefits will be considered in more detail as specific methodologies are considered.

Potential challenges of online data collection

Although the Internet has many potential advantages for data collection, there are also problems and pitfalls that can arise when conducting online research. In the following sub-sections a number of potential issues are identified and discussed. Researchers should consider the extent to which each or any of these issues is relevant to their own research study and how best to address each challenge.

Representativeness

The representativeness of a sample may pose a problem for online research. It has been argued that as the number of Internet users continues to grow, the diversity of online samples should increasingly approximate that of the entire population (Hewson *et al.*, 1996). However, participants recruited online might not be representative of any particular sample group because Internet access is not equally distributed across the population (Granello & Wheaton, 2004;

BOX 1.2   Example of research about the Internet using the Internet

Summary of research from Malik & Coulson (2010b). 'They all supported me but I felt like I suddenly didn't belong anymore': an exploration of perceived disadvantages to online support seeking. *Journal of Psychosomatic Obstetrics & Gynecology,* 31(3), 140–149.

Background

In recent years a growing number of people have been turning to the internet for information, advice and psychosocial support. In the context of infertility, a growing number of couples facing this challenge are engaging in peer support through participation in online self-help and support groups. While a range of positive benefits has been identified, there is comparatively little known about the downside or disadvantages surrounding this increasingly popular type of online support. The aim of this study was therefore to identify the perceived disadvantages to online support seeking in the context of infertility.

Method

An online survey was developed, and with the permission of online support group moderators, it was posted to several infertility online groups. Participants were briefed as to the nature of the study and provided consent through mandatory responding to several key statements outlining the nature of the research and their rights in terms of ethical conduct.

Findings

Over half of the sample (57.9%) reported experiencing disadvantages to online support. Content analysis revealed that the most commonly cited disadvantages were: reading about negative experiences (10.9%), reading about other peoples' pregnancies (8.8%), inaccurate information (7.8%) and it was considered addictive (5.8%). These results suggest that there are many perceived disadvantages to online infertility support groups.

Conclusions

While some of these disadvantages reflect fears commonly cited in the literature, there are also unique disadvantages associated with the experience of infertility and its treatment. The study highlights a number of important areas in which health professionals and community moderators could intervene to better support and improve the online experiences of patients experiencing infertility.

Holtz, Kronberger, & Wagner, 2012). According to recent data, Internet use varies from one country to another (Internet World Stats, 2013), and is influenced by socio-demographic factors like age, gender, income and educational level (Office for National Statistics, 2014), and qualitative differences in patterns of Internet use may also be important (Brandtzæg et al., 2011). Additionally, participants recruited online typically form a self-selected sample because the individual chooses whether or not to take part in the study, and self-selected samples may not generalize to the wider population (Birnbaum, 2004). At present, there appears to be no known technique that researchers can use to recruit a truly random sample of Internet users (Kraut et al., 2004). This is more of a problem for studies that use a translational or novel approach to research rather than a phenomenological approach, which is inherently concerned with online behaviour (Skitka & Sargis, 2006).

Participant anonymity and deception

The anonymity of the Internet poses several challenges when conducting psychological research online. Researchers are likely to be seen as authority figures (Orne, 1962) and in experiment 7 of his investigation into obedience, Stanley Milgram reported that individuals are less likely to obey an authority figure who is not actually physically present in the room (Milgram, 1977). This has implications for online data collection, because not having a researcher in attendance leads to several possibilities for unintentional or deliberate deception by participants. For example, a participant could complete the study more than once, participants could give misleading responses because they have misunderstood the task or they are misbehaving, a group of individuals could sit together at the computer discussing their responses or taking turns to answer questions and then submit their data as if they were a single person, or participants could conceal their real identity and pretend to be somebody else while taking part (Nosek, Banaji, & Greenwald, 2002).

Lower response rates

Response rates can be difficult to calculate for online studies. When conducting traditional paper and pencil surveys, response rates can be calculated by comparing how many questionnaires were distributed with how many were returned. However, on the Internet it may be less clear how many people learned about a study but chose not to take part (Hamilton & Bowers, 2006). Some studies have reported little difference in response rates between online and offline methods (e.g. Whitehead, 2011), but overall it appears that online studies produce lower response rates than other methods of data collection (Manfreda, Bosniak, Berzelak, Haas, & Vehovar, 2008; Shih & Fan, 2009; Yarger et al., 2013). Furthermore, dropout rates can also be higher for online research because participants can leave the study at any time by closing the web browser on their computer, without the embarrassment or social pressure associated with standing up and telling the researcher that they would like to withdraw (Birnbaum, 2004).

Loss of control over research environment

When conducting online studies, the researcher loses control over the environment in which data collection takes place. With laboratory studies the researcher can confirm the identity, age and gender of each participant, tailor instructions to their individual needs, monitor their behaviour to ensure they are fully engaged with the experiment, and intervene if any undesirable effects arise as a result of taking part in the study (Kraut et al., 2004). Researchers can also control the laboratory environment to minimize distractions, avoid unnecessary complications and make sure that the experiment is carried out in a consistent way for all participants (Nosek et al., 2002). However, this level of monitoring and control is not possible when conducting psychological research over the Internet (Kraut *et al.*, 2004). Participants may take part from home, during a break at work, or from a public place like a library or Internet café, they might be alone or with friends, they could be simultaneously doing other things like looking after children or listening to music, they might be distracted midway through the study by the doorbell or telephone, or they could be smoking, eating or drinking at the same time as taking part (Nosek *et al.*, 2002). The appearance of online experiments can also vary depending on the type of computer, monitor, speakers and web browser software used by each participant, leading to a further lack of control. For example, colours might be displayed differently on the screen to what was intended, and individual participants may have the brightness on their computer monitor set to different levels (Birnbaum, 2004).

Stimulus constraints

Online data collection places technical constraints on what kind of studies can be conducted. Although visual and auditory stimuli can be presented over the Internet, it is not possible to use the Internet to conduct research that involves exposing participants to stimuli involving the senses of touch, taste or smell, and participants' auditory and visual responses cannot be recorded without using special equipment (Skitka & Sargis, 2006).

Technical problems

Technical problems while using computers can disrupt data collection and potentially lead to the partial or complete loss of data for some participants. Power failures can cause problems if participants are using a desktop computer without an uninterruptable power supply, or if they have a laptop computer but the battery is not fully charged. Non-working Internet connections can also cause problems, potentially making it impossible for some participants to begin or complete the study. If a computer becomes infected with a virus during data collection then this could disrupt the study and lead to the potential virus-induced loss of any data that has already been collected. Even the type of computer used can potentially be problematic if data is collected in a laboratory rather than the participant's home. Some participants might be familiar with how to use a mouse but not a touchpad, and different screen sizes may cause difficulties for participants who suffer from some form of visual impairment (Benfield & Szlemko, 2006). Additionally, participants might be using an old computer that doesn't have enough memory, an obsolete operating system, an out-of-date web browser that does not support sophisticated features, or a slow dial-up Internet connection that takes a long time to download the experiment and upload their data, all of which could make their computer more likely to crash (Granello & Wheaton, 2004).

Data preparation

Data preparation can also pose some unexpected issues. One of the advantages of working with electronic data is that data is automatically generated and stored on the computer, eliminating the risk of introducing errors while manually entering data. However, the data might need to be transformed or converted into a different format before it can be used, and this could lead to mistakes being made. For example, it might be necessary to convert data from string format into numerical format, or transform Likert scales so they have a scale of 1–5 instead of 0–4 (Benfield & Szlemko, 2006).

Ethical issues in online research

While the Internet has undoubtedly created many new and exciting opportunities for psychological research, it has also introduced new challenges with regards ethical conduct and adherence to ethical principles. As we shall see throughout this textbook, online research can adopt many different designs and as such, may present specific issues to consider and challenges to resolve, some of which may not be readily obvious. However, an important point to note for researchers using online methods is that the ethical issues raised through online research are not unique to the Internet. In fact, the ethical issues raised relate back to the main ethical issues inherent in conducting research with human participants (British Psychological Society, 2013). The challenge for researchers using online methods is to consider how these ethical principles are applied in the context of their own research. Therefore, a useful starting point for us is to consider the main ethical principles underpinning research involving human participants.

According to the British Psychological Society in their Code of Human Research Ethics (2010), there are four main principles that guide our ethical conduct in research (see Box 1.3 for a fuller description). These are:

1. Respect for the autonomy and dignity of persons
2. Scientific value
3. Social responsibility
4. Maximizing benefit and minimizing harm

While there exists a range of ethics guidelines for using online research methods (e.g. Association of Internet Researchers, 2012), these do not necessarily map on to the ethical principles underpinning the field of psychology. Rather, it is recommended that psychologists planning on using online methods to conduct their research refer to the guidelines issued by the British Psychological Society (2013). These guidelines were produced to help researchers as well as ethics committees develop and evaluate research protocols, and to facilitate ethical decision-making in the context of research designs using a range of online methods. According to these guidelines (British Psychological Society, 2013), there are a number of ethical issues arising from the use of online research methods that need to be considered by researchers. These will now be summarized in relation to each of the respective ethical principles that were described in Box 1.3, and which reflect the core values and standards for research involving human participants.

Key ethical questions arising from online research

Ethical Principle 1: Respect for autonomy and dignity of persons

a) *Public/private space* – to what extent can the data obtained from online sources be considered as being in the public or private domain?

Researchers have many different sources of online information potentially at their disposal for the purposes of research and this raises complex issues in relation to privacy. If we consider the

BOX 1.3 Ethical principles for conducting research with human participants

Respect for autonomy and dignity of persons

According to the British Psychological Society *'Psychologists value the dignity and worth of all persons equally, with sensitivity to the dynamics of perceived authority or influence over others and with particular regard to people's rights including those of privacy and self-determination'* (British Psychological Society Code of Ethics and Conduct, 2009, p. 10). As a consequence, psychologists should have a clear duty to participants and should respect the knowledge, expertise and experience of participants (or potential participants) as well as their background socio-demographic characteristics (e.g. gender, ethnicity, socio-economic status, sexual orientation). Psychologists should explain the nature of their research and should avoid any unfair or discriminatory behaviour with regards participant selection or in the content of the research itself. Psychologists should accept that individuals may decline to be involved in research or may subsequently request that data is destroyed. Where there is a time limit on data withdrawal (i.e. the point of data aggregation) then this should be clearly explained. Psychologists should respect the autonomy of individuals by making reasoned judgments about any actions arising from the research. Furthermore, they should respect the privacy of individuals and ensure that they are not personally identifiable, unless in exceptional circumstances and then this should be done using clear and unambiguous informed consent. Psychologists should respect confidentiality and ensure that information or data collected about an individual is appropriately anonymized and cannot be traced back to them, even if the individual is not concerned about a possible loss of confidentiality.

Scientific value

Research should only be undertaken that has been reviewed, designed and conducted in a way that ensures its quality, integrity and contribution to the development of knowledge and understanding. Psychologists should ensure that the scientific and scholarly standards of their research are accountable and of high quality and robustness.

Moreover, judgments of scientific value must be appropriate to the context in which the research is being conducted (e.g. status of the research – student, lecturer, professor).

Social responsibility

Psychology as a discipline exists within the context of society and as such psychologists have a shared duty to ensure the welfare of humans. Psychologists should acknowledge the evolution of social structures in relation to societal need and be respectful of such structures. Psychological knowledge should be generated for beneficial purposes and these can be roughly defined as those that support and reflect the dignity and integrity of individuals but also contribute to the 'common good'. Psychologists need to be able to work with others, be reflective and consider how their research contributes to wider society.

Maximizing benefit and minimizing harm

Psychologists should ensure they maximize the benefits of their work at all stages. Psychologists should consider all research from the perspective of the individual with the aim of avoiding potential risks to well-being, psychological health, mental health, personal values or dignity. If risks are possible then rigorous risk assessment procedures and protocols should be put in place. Typically, the risk of harm should be no greater than in everyday life. However, where there is uncertainty with regards the legitimate needs of the research and the avoidance of risk, reasoned judgement should be applied. If additional and unavoidable risks are likely then they should be assessed in terms of severity and probability and measures put in place to obviate, minimize and manage them. Psychologists should be mindful at all times about the potential impact of their research and ensure that participants are not unwittingly upset or distressed. They also need to be aware of the power imbalance that may exist and should be sensitive to the needs of participants at all times. In essence, the psychologist must consider the costs to the participant in relation to the benefits to society and while this is not an easy judgment to make, it should be done so with due care, diligence and thorough analysis.

guidance from the Code of Human Research Ethics (2010), we find that the observation of public behaviour can only occur in instances where those who are being observed 'would expect to be observed by strangers' (p. 25). This would suggest that all research observing individuals in situations where they would not expect to be observed as prohibited. What does this mean for online research? This is an important issue for researchers engaging in online research since it is fair to say that the distinction between private and public has become increasingly vague. Moreover, it is difficult to know exactly what people might consider is 'private' and what they feel is 'public' in relation to their online activities. For example, an individual who is a member of an online discussion forum might read and post messages while at home. In this example, the communication is taking place in a private setting (i.e. home) and a public one (i.e. discussion forum). Researchers should be mindful of the ways in which individuals engage with the Internet and try and appreciate the fact that some individuals might consider their online communications to be private, despite the fact that they were made to a seemingly public discussion forum as well as agreeing to the Internet service providers' End User Licence Agreements.

In order to resolve this issue, researchers should consider the extent to which the online information being considered as data for a study, or the undisclosed observation of an individual, may have a negative impact upon them and use this as a basis for deciding whether valid consent is necessary. In the context of the aforementioned example, one potential solution might be to consider liaising with a discussion forum moderator to seek permission to undertake the study.

At the end of the day, the researcher needs to make a judgement call based on these ethical considerations and may conclude that use of research data obtained online from individuals without valid consent is acceptable.

b) *Confidentiality* – to what extent is there a risk to the confidentiality of an individual's data? If we think these risks are likely, how can they be minimized and how should we inform participants of the risks?

Following on from the issues raised in (a) Public/private space, researchers should always seek to ensure that any data obtained online remains confidential. This should be the case during all stages of the research including dissemination, such as dissertations, scientific papers and conference presentations. One of the challenges facing researchers concerns the traceability of online data. Indeed, it is not always immediately obvious to researchers just how easy it may be to trace a piece of online data. However, there may be instances when this issue is more obvious and an example may be when a researcher includes a quote from a discussion forum member or publishes data from the source. In such cases, it is relatively easy to submit the data (e.g. quote) to a search engine and to be taken directly to the discussion forum and the original message posted. Researchers in such instances should reflect carefully on whether such actions compromise the confidentiality and anonymity of the individual who generated the original data and whether valid consent should be sought. Furthermore, the extent to which the tracing of quotes back to the source individual may pose subsequent harm should be considered. In instances where any potential harm is deemed serious, then researchers may wish to consider an alternative approach. One suggestion may be to paraphrase or combine quotes in publications, but before submitting them for publication or dissemination checking to see whether the quote can be traced. However, depending on the specific research question and design employed, this may or may not be a satisfactory solution.

c) *Copyright* – what are the copyright issues? Who owns the data? When should permission be sought to use potential sources of data for research?

   A particularly difficult issue, at times, is that of copyright and legal aspects concerning the use of data derived from the public domain. Researchers should be aware that copyright often rests with the author or web hosting company. In particular, 'public' material from social networking sites often rests with the web hosting service, as does the communication between members that has been mediated by the web service provider. Researchers should always be aware of these legislative issues and consider whether permission should be obtained to use such online data. Online, only such 'data' that is not protected by copyright can truly be said to be in the public domain.

d) *Valid consent* – what procedures need to be put in place to ensure valid, robust and traceable consent?

   In such cases where it is concluded by the researcher that the online data pertinent to a specific study is not in the public domain, or that undisclosed use of such data cannot be argued on scientific grounds, then valid consent should be sought. However, obtaining valid consent is not always a straightforward endeavour and there are a number of things that can be done to try and ensure valid consent has been obtained. For example, in the context of an online survey, researchers should include an information page clearly explaining the nature of the study, what is expected of the participant and their ethical rights (see Appendix A). In addition, potential participants should be made aware of any potential risks that may arise as a result of engaging with the study. Furthermore, it is recommended that following this information there is a section addressing issues of consent. This is perhaps best achieved by having a small (i.e. 3–5) number of consent statements that must be agreed to (i.e. by 'ticking' their agreement) before proceeding to the actual data collection phase of the survey (see Appendix B).

e) *Withdrawal* – what procedures need to be put in place to allow participants to enact their right to withdraw their data?

Participants must have the right to withdraw from the study at any point including after they have participated and relevant instructions should be provided including any time restriction on when this can be done (e.g. removal of data following completion of a survey can be done up until 14 days post completion). However, in the context of online research there are additional considerations and challenges facing the researcher. For example, a participant might decide to withdraw from a study midway through. The challenge facing the researcher is how they know that this has happened, especially if data has already been submitted and stored. One simple solution might be, in the context of a survey, to include an exit button on each page. By clicking this exit button, participants could be taken to a short debriefing page that may include questions about whether they wish any data submitted thus far to be removed. However, the extent to which such exit buttons can be used may well be dependent upon the survey software package being used (see Section 'Online software packages').

f) *Debriefing* – what procedures needs to be in place to debrief participants?

Researchers may need to consider how best to ensure that participants have been fully debriefed following engagement with their online study. In the context of the online survey, this may be relatively straightforward in as much as a de-briefing page can be displayed at the end of the survey (see Appendix C). However, ensuring that participants have fully read and understood this information may be an important consideration. In such instances, researchers may wish to include a statement asking participants to confirm they have read the material and are happy with what it says.

Ethical Principle 2: Scientific value

g) *Levels of control* – how might reduced levels of control impact on the scientific value of the study? How can levels of control be maximized?

Again, researchers should consider the core ethical principles as articulated in the Code of Human Research Ethics (2010), and in doing so the importance of quality, integrity and contribution will be evident. That is to say, researchers using online methods may wish to consider how the particular methods chosen impact upon these issues, especially in terms of control. By control, we are talking about the extent to which the researcher is able to have oversight over the behaviour of the research participants, characteristics and the research process.

In the context of online research, the issue of control is perhaps more salient due to the distance between the researcher and the study participant. In the Ethics Guidelines for Internet-mediated Research (British Psychological Society, 2013), four issues were identified as being problematic: (1) who has access to participate in the research study; (2) the environmental conditions in which the participants are engaging with the research; (3) the feelings, thoughts, perceptions and emotions of the participants; and (4) variations in the research process as a result of different hardware and software configurations.

Ethical Principle 3: Social responsibility

h) *Disruption of social structures* – to what extent does the study procedures and dissemination plans disrupt or harm social groups?

Researchers using online methods should carefully consider all aspects of their work, not least the potential intrusion or disruption of social structures as well as how their research dissemination plans might impact on participants. For example, researchers wishing to examine social networking sites or online discussion forums may well need to consider this issue in some depth. Indeed, in doing so many of the issues and arguments outlined earlier concerning the distinction between private and public space may be relevant. Members of online discussion forums may well react badly to an uninvited intrusion and may consider the actions of the researcher to be a violation of their private space. However, the issues raised here will largely depend on the specific research questions and scientific value of the research study. It may be argued by the researcher that an uninvited and undisclosed venture into an online discussion forum is warranted, and in such instances robust justifications will be required.

These issues are also pertinent to the dissemination activities planned for the research study. For example, a research report made available through open access may contain details and information about an online discussion forum and unwanted attention may be directed towards it from readers of the report. Indeed, issues of anonymity and confidentiality are particularly relevant in this scenario and researchers should be mindful of these as they plan for future publication and other dissemination of their work. These issues should also be considered even if the outcome is a research dissertation likely to sit on the shelf of a university library.

Ethical Principle 4: Maximizing benefits and minimizing harm

i) *Maximizing benefits* – How might all the aforementioned issues impact upon the maximization of benefits? What procedures need to be put in place to maximize the benefits from a piece of research?

As the researcher plans and designs their online research study, many of the issues already identified and discussed earlier in this section will be pertinent. Indeed, it is often the case that in preparing their study protocol for ethical approval that these issues will require explicit discussion in order to satisfy the ethics standards being considered by review boards and ethics committees.

j) *Minimizing harm* – How might all the aforementioned issues lead to potential harm to participants? What procedures need to be put in place to reduce the likelihood of participants being harmed?

For researchers, the challenge is to consider how these issues may be relevant to their own specific study at all stages of the research process. In addressing the issues already mentioned, it is hoped that the researcher will be undertaking a study that has sought to maximize benefit and minimize harm. Indeed, it is often the weighing of these issues that poses the greatest challenge for researchers. Moreover, researchers should always seek to reflect on their professional obligations and consider such ethical issues from the outset. Conceivably, this may lead to instances where a number of ethical issues arising from the online nature of the study could not be resolved. In such cases, researchers may wish to ask themselves whether the online nature of their proposed investigation is indeed the correct one. For example, perhaps the topic is highly personal or sensitive or perhaps the age of participants cannot be guaranteed (i.e. over 16s) and so the decision is made to use offline methods instead.

In summary, the issue of ethical decision-making in the context of online research is a very important one and such a brief coverage would not do this issue justice. Therefore, researchers should seek to examine other literature pertaining to both offline and online methods and consider all issues pertinent to their own research study. However, in doing so, researchers should not lose sight of the fact that the same core ethical principles underpin research using both offline and online methods, as described in the Code of Human Research Ethics (2010). It is not the case that the issues are widely different but rather it is about the application and interpretation of these principles in the context of the online nature of the study. Having said that, it is unlikely to be the case that such considerations and reflections will be straightforward. However, if researchers consider these core principles carefully and keep them uppermost in their thinking then there is a greater likelihood that sound and ethically acceptable decisions will be made.

How to behave online

For those new to online research, there are a number of rules and informal standards that users of the Internet adhere to in order to interact with other users in a socially acceptable and agreeable manner. This is called 'netiquette' and will be the topic of the next section.

Netiquette

In each culture, there is a system of rules that might not be explicitly stated but which are expected and enforced nevertheless. For someone entering into a new culture, there is a chance that they may commit a few social blunders unless they know the rules. For example, it might be easy to cause offence or perhaps to misunderstand what others have said and take offence when none was intended.

Online these rules are intrinsically different to those of everyday life. The online environment is novel and many of the tools that we might use to communicate with one another are not applicable. For example, we cannot use facial expressions, the tone of voice, laughter or body language to help us. Moreover, while online it can be all too easy to forget that we are actually talking to another, real life human being. So, in order to assist those researchers who may be unfamiliar with online behaviour or particular aspects of it, the rules of netiquette are worth considering.

The term 'netiquette' is a combination of the words 'net' (from Internet) and 'etiquette'. In essence, it refers to a set of social conventions that facilitate interaction over networks. While much has been written about online behaviour, Virginia Shea's (1994) *Netiquette* offers an easy and straightforward set of rules that researchers should keep in mind as they undertake online research. These 11 rules are summarized below:

Rule 1: Remember the human

The golden rule to remember when conducting oneself online is to never forget that the person reading your mail or posting is, indeed, a person, with feelings that can be hurt. Indeed, when communicating online (i.e. via PC, mobile phone or tablet), it is all too easy to forget that those are real people out there with real feelings and egos. A useful rule of thumb is as follows: if you wouldn't say something to their face – you should not say it over the Internet.

Rule 2: Adhere to the same standards of behaviour online that you follow in real life

Online it is very easy to forget that there is a human being on the other side of the computer screen, and some people might believe that a lower standard of ethics or personal behaviour is acceptable in cyberspace. This is absolutely not the case. While online the research should always be ethical. Netiquette mandates that you do your best to act within the laws of society and the online environment.

Rule 3: Know where you are in cyberspace

Netiquette varies from domain to domain (i.e. chat rooms, blogs, etc.) so what is acceptable in one area may not be in another. When you enter a domain of cyberspace that is new to you, take a look around to get a sense of the culture and how people conduct themselves before actively participating.

Rule 4: Respect other people's time

Remember, when you send an email or post a message to a discussion group, you are taking up someone else's time. People have less time than ever today, precisely because they have so much information to absorb. It is your responsibility to ensure that the time they spend reading your posting is not wasted. Some basic guidelines to posting are:

- Post messages to the appropriate discussion group
- Read the FAQ (Frequently Asked Questions) document before asking questions
- When appropriate, use private email instead of posting to the group to reply to blogs, postings, etc.

Rule 5: Make yourself look good online

Take advantage of your anonymity; but remember you will be judged by the quality of your writing. Pay attention to the content of your writing. Be sure you know what you are talking about. In addition, make sure your notes are clear, logical, and grammatically correct. Be pleasant and polite and don't use offensive language.

Rule 6: Share expert knowledge

If you are an expert, don't be afraid to share what you know. Online, people are searching for knowledgeable answers to various questions, so if you have information to share, what better venue to share your expertise!

Rule 7: Help keep flame wars under control

'Flaming' is what people do when they express a strongly held opinion without holding back any emotion. Flames can be lots of fun, both to write and to read. Netiquette does, however, forbid the continuation of a series of angry letters, which can dominate the tone and destroy the friendship of a discussion, as it is unfair to the other members of the group.

Rule 8: Respect other people's privacy

It is always a common courtesy to respect other's privacy, including personal information shared via blogs, web pages, messages, etc.

Rule 9: Don't abuse your power

Knowing more than others, or having more power than they do, does not give you the right to take advantage of them. You should never use your power to violate others privacy by reading personal emails, etc.

Rule 10: Be forgiving of other people's mistakes

Everyone was a newbie at one point in time. When someone makes a mistake, give the individual the benefit of the doubt. When someone makes a mistake, a spelling error, a stupid question or an unnecessarily long answer, you should be polite when pointing it out.

Rule 11: All Caps is considered 'shouting'

Using all caps (i.e. USING ALL CAPS) is considered 'shouting'. If you want to stress a word, surround the word with asterisks (*).

Chapter summary

In this chapter we have introduced the role Internet as a potential research tool for psychologists. As can be seen from the brief historical introduction, the Internet and its capabilities have grown exponentially and are likely to continue to do so in the future. For researchers, such technological advancements create new opportunities as well as challenges. We have considered a number of potential benefits to researchers not only in terms of access, convenience and efficiency but also in new social phenomenon to be studied. However, there are a number of challenges facing researchers and these have been outlined, though the extent to which they present a serious issue will of course depend on the precise nature of the study being undertaken. However, regardless of the particular topic being investigated, all researchers will need to consider the ethical issues arising from their work. As we have seen, researchers should not be mistaken for thinking that ethical issues pertaining to online research are unique to that medium, in fact it is the contrary. Researchers, regardless of whether they engage with offline or online methods, must consider their research studies using the same core ethical principles. However, for those researchers engaged with online methods the challenge becomes one of applying and interpreting these principles in the context of the specific online methodology (e.g. online survey, focus group or discussion forum) being used. Indeed, researchers may find this a difficult and challenging task and no 'right answer' may be evident. The key to success, as it were, rests in making as ethically sound a judgement as possible by considering all the appropriate and pertinent ethical considerations raised by the specific research project. In conclusion to this chapter, we considered a set of user-friendly guidelines that is called 'netiquette' that should help researchers engage politely and professionally with study participants online. In the following chapters, we shall consider specific online methods in detail and examine their use in psychological research.

Further reading

Association of Internet Researchers (2012). *Ethical decision making and internet research*. Available to download from http://aoir.org/reports/ethics2.pdf.

British Psychological Society (2009). *Code of ethics and conduct*. Leicester, UK: British Psychological Society.

British Psychological Society (2010). *Code of human research ethics*. Leicester, UK: British Psychological Society.

British Psychological Society (2013). *Ethics guidelines for conducting Internet-mediated research*. Leicester, UK: British Psychological Society.

Kraut, R., Olson, J., Banaji, M., Bruckman, A., Cohen, J. & Couper, N. (2004). Psychological research online: report of the Board of Scientific Affairs' Advisory Group on the conduct of research on the Internet. *American Psychologist, 59*(2), 105–117.

Skitka, L. J. & Sargis, E. G. (2006). The Internet as psychological laboratory. *Annual Review of Psychology, 57,* 529–555.

2 **Online Interviews**

This chapter begins by providing a brief discussion of the role of the interview in psychological research and its key features. Opportunities for online interviews are then discussed with a range of advantages as well as challenges identified. Next, the chapter describes the most popular types of synchronous and asynchronous online interviews available to researchers, namely those done via email and instant messenger. The chapter explores the key features of both these types of online interview and provides some useful strategies to undertake successful online interviews.

Interviews

A popular data collection tool within psychology has been the qualitative interview and has been used for many decades. Kvale (1983) defined the qualitative research interview as 'an interview, whose purpose is to gather descriptions of the life-world of the interviewee with respect to interpretation of the meaning of described phenomena' (p. 174). Such interviews have historically been undertaken either face-to-face or to a lesser extent via telephone. For researchers undertaking the interview face-to-face there is the benefit of being able to use its social cues to facilitate the process. For example, the voice, intonation and body language can all assist the researcher to understand the thoughts, feelings and experiences of the participant with regards the topic of the interview. Indeed, for some topics, such as personal or upsetting issues, it may be especially helpful in judging whether the interview should be paused or terminated.

Additionally, in face-to-face interviews there is no significant delay between the question that is posed by the researcher and each can directly react to what the other has said. As a consequence, the face-to-face interview is often seen to be a spontaneous interaction, without any lengthy periods of participant or researcher reflection. The researcher is therefore required to focus more on this inter-action and the answers that are being provided. In the semi-structured or unstructured interview format, the researcher has to develop questions based on the responses provided and this can be a challenging task at times.

Face-to-face and telephone interviews can be audiotaped, with permission, and this has the advantage that the transcript is more accurate than simply writing notes. However, researchers often fail to keep any notes at all because they are audiotaping the interview. However, interview notes may in fact be helpful in the subsequent data analysis, particularly if the audiotape turns out to be of poor quality.

In the face-to-face interview the researcher also has the oppor-tunity to develop rapport and put the participant at ease and this may be achieved partly through conducting the interview at a convenient venue (e.g. home, workplace). However, this scenario may present a number of time and resource implications and where significant travel is involved then the demands on the researcher may be considerable.

Finally, in the face-to-face interview the researcher is able to close out the interview easily and ensure that the participant is happy with the process (partly through assessing non-verbal communi-cation). The researcher is able to check that the participant has said everything that they wish to say or whether there are any final comments and remarks they would like to make.

Online interviews

As with other research methodologies described in this textbook, the Internet has presented new opportunities for qualitative researchers to engage in the interview process. However, it is fair to say that there exists a divergence of opinion with regards the role of the Internet in undertaking qualitative interviews and suit-ability for psychological research. While Ayling and Mewse (2009) argue that 'online qualitative research is valuable in its own right, and that the advantages considerably outweigh the difficulties' (p. 575), an alternative position is presented by Davis *et al.* (2004)

who state that 'online synchronous interviews do not readily lend themselves to the exploration of meaning' (p. 951).

It would seem that for researchers wishing to consider the Internet as a vehicle to conduct their qualitative interviews, considerable attention should be given to the practical, ethical and methodological issues raised by online interviewing. As we have seen in the previous chapter, there are not only several issues to consider and challenges to address but also many potential benefits to the research process as well. Essentially, it is up to each researcher in the context of their study to reflect upon these issues and make an informed decision as to the best way to proceed. However, for those considering the online interview, the following sections offer some useful insights into their advantages and challenges, as well as types of online interviews that can be conducted and helpful guidance on how to get the most out of this form of data collection methodology. However, before we turn our attention to specific types of online interviews it is worth mentioning that many of the advantages (e.g. cost, timing and location, accessing hard to reach populations, anonymity, reduction in unequal power relationships, digital record) and challenges (e.g. drop out, non-verbal information) discussed in previous chapter are also relevant considerations in the context of online interviews. However, rather than simply repeating that which has been said already, this chapter will only raise selected issues relevant to specific types of online interview formats.

Types of online interviews

Broadly speaking, there are two main types of online interviews that reflect whether the researcher and participant are communicating in real-time (synchronous) or not (asynchronous). Asynchronous online interviews do not need the researcher and participant to be online at the same time and to date the most popular medium through which to conduct this type of interview is via email. In contrast, the synchronous online interview requires both the researcher and participant to be present online at the same time with text-based conversation typically being undertaken via instant messaging (IM) or chat software. As we will pick up again in Chapter 3, the decision as to whether to engage in synchronous or asynchronous online communication may be relatively straightforward or it may be more difficult with many factors to consider. Researchers must carefully consider the needs of their project together with the specific advantages and challenges raised by each of these types of communication tools used in online interviewing.

In the following two sections we shall consider each of these types of online interview and reflect upon their key features and implications for the qualitative research interview process.

Asynchronous online interviews using email

In an effort to describe what is meant by asynchronous online interviewing using email, it is perhaps best to state what it is not. First of all, it is not to be confused with an email survey (see Chapter 4), as the interview is typically semi-structured in nature and consists of multiple email messages being sent between the researcher and participant over a period of time (e.g. few days or weeks). Similarly, asynchronous online interviewing using email is not to be confused with asynchronous focus groups (see Chapter 3). That is, the answers offered by interview participants are not made available to other participants and are therefore not shared, viewed or influenced by other research participants.

Many of the potential advantages or challenges surrounding the use of asynchronous online interviews using email are similar to those arising from other online methods and which will be discussed in later chapters, however, there are a number of particularly important issues which merit discussion in the present chapter.

Efficiency

While email interviews may carry significant financial savings for researchers, in comparison to face-to-face or telephone interviews, they are also efficient in terms of eliminating the need for transcription since the interview is already in electronic format and may only need a little editing before analysis can begin. One important feature of the email interview is the fact that several interviews can be conducted simultaneously and so there is no need to arrange a specific set time and date. This may be something that is especially helpful to researchers as they can send a set of questions to participants at the same time.

The amount of time required by participants to respond to and send back their answers may vary considerably. For example, Meho (2006) found in a review of email interviews that some studies reported a delay of several months before all the data is collected, whereas others reported having received it within a week.

The actual amount of time it requires to undertake a research study using email may vary markedly and this is due to a number of issues including the number of participants required, number of questions to be asked, degree of motivation and engagement by participants, the amount of data and its quality, the time available by both researchers and participants as well as the obvious access to the Internet.

Effects of the medium

One of the most important differences between the email interview and the face-to-face interview concerns the ability to facilitate interaction and feedback and the ability to communicate using multiple senses (Panteli, 2002). As a result, the 'richest' data may be regarded as that obtained via face-to-face interviews, followed by telephone interviews with email interviews last. However, this may be too simplistic a view since the email interview may be helpful in terms of eliminating the effects of any differences between the participant and the researcher (e.g. gender, age, ethnicity, disability, dress and so on). Indeed, Egan *et al.* (2006) discussed how there was an expectation that traumatic brain injury survivors would not be able to or wish to engage with the email interview process but in reality it proved to be very successful for some of the reasons already outlined (see Box 2.1). Furthermore, the email interview may also be helpful in terms of facilitating disclosure and encouraging participants to share personal experiences, opinions or viewpoints that might be more difficult in the face-to-face context. Indeed, Kim *et al.* (2003) argue that, among other things, email may help reassure and make participants feel safe and thereby allow them to raise issues that might be difficult to discuss (e.g. family relationships and conflict, racism, academic problems). Similarly, Griffiths (2010) considered the asynchronous online interview to be helpful in the context of interviewing gamblers and gaming addicts. As he notes, 'the main advantage of interviewing gaming addicts online is that for the person being interviewed it may overcome feelings of embarrassment, alienation and stigmatization particularly as addictions to gambling or video games can be difficult and sensitive subjects to talk about.' (p. 16).

One challenge for researchers wishing to use the email interview in their research arises from the fact that some potential participants may not be very good at typing (Note: this issue is especially problematic for synchronous online interviews, see Section 'Synchronous online interviews using instant messaging'). However, it must be acknowledged that the opposite problem may in fact be the case, that is, some individuals may be much more comfortable talking online than in face-to-face.

Interview questions

Researchers using the email interview have a choice as to how many of their questions they may wish to share with participants. Some researchers share all the questions at the outset, sometimes even with the email invitation in order to be clear about what is being asked. Others, however, might send only a question at a time or a handful of questions around a common issue. It is fair to say that there are no right or wrong approaches or standardized procedures for email interviews, therefore researchers should consider the pros and cons of how many questions to give participants in each email sent. Pilot work may be especially useful here in helping determine the most appropriate strategy since the preferences of one target population may differ markedly from those of another.

Regardless of the number of questions, researchers should consider how best to send the questions. That is, whether messages are embedded within an email message or via email attachment (the latter issue is considered in more depth in Section 'Email surveys'). The evidence suggests that the former may be more helpful in terms of response rate and in fact Dommeyer & Moriarty (2000) suggest it is five times as much.

Perhaps one of the most helpful benefits to participants is the fact that they can engage with the interview in a familiar and convenient environment, such as at home or work or using their mobile

BOX 2.1 Example of asynchronous online interviews using email

Summary of research from Egan, J., Chenoweth, L. & McAuliffe, D. (2006). Email-facilitated qualitative interviews with traumatic brain injury survivors: a new and accessible method. *Brain Injury*, 20(12), 1283–1294.

Background

This paper reports on the role of the email interview with individuals who have a traumatic brain injury (TBI) and was part of a wider research project exploring the role of the Internet for such individuals.

Rationale for the email interview

The authors note that qualitative research in the field of TBI is under-represented. A number of unique aspects of this condition may, in part, explain this fact. For example, face-to-face interviews are largely language dependent and reply on responses from participants in 'real-time' thereby precluding time for considered reflection. In the context of TBI, this immediacy is argued to be a key barrier to successful qualitative research and a number of additional issues were identified including: (1) unable to recall events accurately, (2) easily distracted due to noise or interruptions during the interview and the expectation to spontaneously process information and respond to questions, (3) fatigue, (4) difficulties associated with abstract and/or open-ended questions, (5) becoming agitated, reduced fluency and becoming tangential when 'prompted', (6) difficulty focussing because of negative feelings and (7) reluctant to self-disclose because of a need to minimize losses (Paterson & Scott-Findley, 2002).

As a consequence of these aforementioned issues surrounding the use of face-to-face interviewing with TBI patients, the authors proposed the use of email interviews as a means to try and address these challenges. Using a semi-structured interview format, and after piloting, the authors undertook email interviews with 19 participants (12 males, 7 females) aged 21–64 years with the majority (*N* = 17) having a severe TBI.

Observations by the researchers

The researchers noted almost immediately that the email interview showed great promise as a means to facilitate engagement in the research process of individuals with TBI. As reported, a number of observations were made:

1. It was noted that rapport was evident with most interviewees very quickly and that conversations resembled 'reflective dialogues' (p. 1287). Furthermore, individuality was noted via differences in grammatical and semantic complexity, humour and use of emoticons as well as style of replies.
2. Nearly all of the interview participants (n = 18) were able to respond to and answer the most abstract questions
3. The quality of the data generated, in many instances, was rich and conveyed insight and humour. Egan *et al.* (2006) noted the response by one patient (17 years post-morbid) with a severe TBI to an abstract question on whether Internet addiction could lead to social isolation. The participant replied '*I can see that it would be possible to become addicted, especially in my instance where I (sic) have no allotted log in periods or dial up charges, and you could miss out on all the physical interactions which take place between individuals in face-to-face communications*' (p. 1287).
4. The participants were able to have more time for reflection and often emailed additional thoughts to earlier answered questions, thereby enhancing the quality of the data.
5. The research team were able to look over the responses provided by participants and this allowed them the opportunity to reflect as well as craft considered responses. In addition, the researchers were able to make appropriate adjustments to the interview schedules in light of this review process.

However, there were some problematic aspects identified. First, sometimes communication did break down between participants and the researcher in terms of misunderstandings surrounding some parts of questions. Second, the interviews took a long time to complete, ranging from 1 to 6 months though they note that these periods do not reflect a sustained period of activity.

Feedback from the participants

Each of the email interview participants were asked for feedback and to respond to a series of questions including: (1) Email interviewing is a fairly new way to do an interview. What do you think of this way to do an interview? (2) Do you think you would have given the same answers in a face-to-face interview as in an email interview?

The feedback from the participants towards the use of email interviews was positive indeed. The authors quote one response from a participant who has engaged in face-to-face research: '*I have been involved in face-to-face interviews with students doing research and have often been feeling overwhelmed, by the number of questions, the depth of the questions and the prodding by the interviewer when giving my replies. Often I have had to ask a number of times what was the actual question. I have needed breaks (because of pain) and the 'not many more' (questions) reply is insulting, it invalidated my feelings and request for a break, like my pain is not as important as their finishing in a certain time frame. Naturally my interest wanes as a result, I want to finish so will bypass questions or be a bit glib in my response*' (p. 1288).

In addition, the participants regarded the email interview as a means of facilitating greater reflection time and control over what personal information is disclosed, particularly that which is difficult to recall. Other participants reported that they felt 'safe' and appreciated the familiarity of the email as a communication tool. Similarly, the text-based nature of the communication also helped those with poorer recall and memory problems in that they could save emails, re-read them and respond when appropriate. Furthermore, participants reported that they felt more able to focus and keep to the point of the interview. Indeed, the asynchronous nature of email meant they could take their time to fully comprehend the question and formulate their responses. For many participants, they felt that they communicated more effectively as a result of using email than they would have done in a face-to-face interview. Among the other comments made by participants was the ease and convenience associated with email communication and the fact they didn't have to travel anywhere and they felt refreshed when engaging in the process rather than fatigued (as might have been the case in face-to-face).

Similar to the research team, participants did note some disadvantages associated with the email interview. For example, some mentioned the challenge of not being able to see or hear someone and so it was difficult to determine if they were genuine and trustworthy. Another participant noted the ease with which an email message can be misunderstood, again as a result of the absence of visual or aural cues. Also, one participant reported that they could not relay their full story since they were slow at typing.

phone. This may be welcomed by participants and allow them to respond to the research questions in their own time. However, this does mean that each question needs to be expressed very clearly and is understandable to participants. In instances where they are not, participants may become frustrated and disengage from the interview.

Data quality

An important issue faced by researchers is whether the data generated through this type of online data collection method is of lesser quality than the traditional face-to-face interview. A number of studies have in fact shed light on this issue as they either compared or conducted both face-to-face interviews as well as email interviews (e.g. Curasi, 2001; Murray, 2004). The findings of such studies revealed that those participants who were interviewed via email appeared to remain more focussed on the interview questions and provided accounts that were richer in reflection as compared with those who engaged in face-to-face interviews. However, it should be noted that while the face-to-face interviews were very successful, the email interviews were especially successful because the participants and researchers were able to take their time and consider their responses carefully before sending their responses (Karchner, 2001; Murray, 2004).

According to Curasi (2001), data quality is driven by a number of factors including who is being interviewed, who is doing the interviewing as well as how much expertise the researchers have with regards to online interviewing. For example, in her work she found that some participants generated only very brief answers to interview questions, whereas others discussed issues and provided very detailed and lengthy responses. In some studies, researchers noted that the data generated through face-to-face interviews did not reveal any information that was not already available via the email interviews. In contrast, some studies have found that some information (e.g. health, medical, political and so on) captured through the email interview was not revealed through the traditional face-to-face interviews (e.g. Beck, 2005; Murray & Sixsmith, 1998).

In summary, asynchronous online interviewing via email provides researchers the opportunity to capture in an engaging and interactive manner, participants' thoughts, feelings and opinions in their own words. Perhaps most importantly is the fact that the email interview empowers the participant, as they are able to take control over when they respond and what they say (Bowker & Tuffin, 2004).

Synchronous online interviews using instant messaging

IM is an online communication tool that supports the exchange of text messages, spoken language and files. Researchers wishing to undertake online synchronous interviewing have many IM services available to them that share many similarities. In essence, a conversation window is displayed on the screen for both the researcher and the participant that keeps a running log of the evolving conversation. Typically, each has a text box that sits below this window and through which they type their message. An important feature of this means of communication is that only once each message has been fully typed is it then uploaded to the conversation window, through clicking a 'submit' button or equivalent. According to Chen & Hinton (1999: 4.3), this process of writing then submitting messages allows for the development of a more ordered and structured conversation where dialogue is composed of textual 'chunks' (i.e. sentences of paragraphs).

There are a number of other features that make IM potentially useful to the researcher. For example, researchers can easily view the online or offline status of participants that are known by their IM usernames. Moreover, many IM programmes offer a public address book service that allows certain profile data to be viewed. From the perspective of the researcher, this may have implications in terms of verifying that the information provided during an IM interview matches the information provided in the IM profile in the address book. An additional potential benefit of the address book is that it could be used as a sampling frame.

As noted by Jowett et al. (2011), there is no real consensus by researchers as to the IM software that is most appropriate to the online interview. However, one important issue raised by Jowett et al. (2011) is that of data security and the risk of personal information being transmitted through an IM service being intercepted by a third party. Indeed, some researchers have employed encrypted chat software (e.g. Ayling & Mewse, 2009), whereas other have simply used software such as private chat rooms contained within websites used by study participants or free software such as Microsoft Messenger© (Couch & Liamputtong, 2008; Davis et al., 2004). A challenge faced by researchers is that of securing data and ensuring participants have the technological skills to download, install and engage with new software. In many instances, interview participants may feel altogether more comfortable and familiar with other software that is in fact less secure and places the transmission of personal data at risk of interception. In their study, Ayling & Mewse (2009) reported that some of their study participants opted not to use encrypted software when given the opportunity but preferred more familiar software, such as Microsoft Messenger©. Moreover, some participants reported that they found installing encrypted software especially difficult. As a consequence, researchers may consider whether the provision of encrypted software is required, however, as Ayling & Mewse (2009) suggested, it need not be given the degree to which participants were unconcerned about data security and the challenges associated with using the specific software.

In a study by Stieger & Göritz (2006), a web-based survey was conducted to explore people's habits with regards use of IM and the reasons they may have to engage in an interview using this medium. The survey respondents ($N = 946$, mean age = 24.1 years, SD = 9.0) were asked to endorse which, from a set of 9 reasons, they agreed with as considerations in deciding whether to engage in an IM scientific interview. The results were as follows: 'I should be told how the researcher got my IM name' (44.4%); 'Exact topic of study should be known in advance' (43.1%); 'My own curiosity' (39.0%); 'Feedback about the results' (38.5%); 'Full anonymity of my answers' (36.1%); 'Contribute to research' (33.2%); 'Possibility to learn something about myself' (25.7%); 'Monetary incentives' (15.1%) and 'The researcher's appeal for help' (11.3%).

In addition, the survey participants were asked what their most likely reaction would be to a chat request to take part in a scientific IM interview. From the 594 who provided a response, 271 (45.6%) said they would participate in the study, 224 (37.7%) said they would ask for further information about the nature of the study, 4 (0.7%) said they would take part but give false answers and 95 (16.0%) reported that they would delete the chat request.

For researchers considering the IM interview as their means of data collection, there are important differences in potential modes of invitations to participate. For example, if an email invitation arrives at a point that is not convenient then the individual may return to it later and reply. However, a chat request in IM is delivered instantaneously to the recipient, regardless of what they are doing. It is likely to be ignored if it is not answered there and then. In addition, individuals may be engaged in another activity or perhaps even another online conversation and the request is ignored. Furthermore, some IM packages allow users to block chat requests from people who are not in the user's buddy list. In this instance, the researcher is not aware that their chat request was not even delivered and the user is not aware that they were sent a chat request.

Guidelines for effective online interviewing

In order to help researchers undertake effective, efficient and fruitful online interviews, the following suggestions are made though researchers should be aware that many of the recommendations given in other chapters may in fact be relevant for this online method also:

1. *Personalized interview invitation:* In keeping with the recommendations made by Dillman (2000), recruit potential participants individually if possible. The rationale being that such an approach makes a potential participant feel important and may benefit the researcher in terms of encouraging them to be interviewed. However, that is not to say that recruitment and invitations should not be attempted through mailing lists or discussion forums, but simply where possible

BOX 2.2 Example of synchronous online interview using instant messaging

Summary of research from Jowett, A., Peel, E. & Shaw, R. (2011). Online interviewing in psychology: reflections on the process. *Qualitative Research in Psychology*, 8(4), 354–369.

Background

The authors conducted an online survey exploring the experiences of non-heterosexuals living with diabetes (see Jowett & Peel, 2009) and invited interested participants to indicate whether they would be willing to be interviewed as part of the project. This paper reports on the experiences of the research team in undertaking these interviews using IM software.

Rationale for the instant messaging interview

As a result of the geographical spread of survey participants who agreed to be interviewed as part of their project, the researchers considered the online interview to be the most viable approach but in order to gather data in a single interaction opted for the IM approach.

Observations by the researchers

In their fascinating paper, the researchers reflect on several key areas surrounding their experience of using IM. These include:

1. The researchers noted the practical challenges facing them as many of the potential interview participants resided in North America. As a consequence, interviews had to be scheduled with time zone differences in mind, but this was not always successfully done. The researchers explain that some participants were confused about specific timings and interviews had to be rescheduled. Furthermore, additional challenges were faced as a result of working patterns that meant that sometimes the researchers were conducting online interviews late in the evening. Interviews conducted at the weekends appeared to be the most convenient.

2. While the researchers were mindful of the time commitment required by participants they noted the fact that previous discussions within the literature may have down played this. In their experience, the interviews

took much longer with an expected 1-hour interview often taking up to 3 hours in reality. As a result of this, the team quite correctly offered participants the opportunity to take breaks or to conduct the interviews over several days but all preferred to complete it in one session. An additional observation was that the actual amount of textual data generated through the interviews was considerably less than expected (i.e. 12,000 words for a face-to-face interviews versus 6,000 for IM interviews).

3. While the research team endeavoured to work with participants to determine the IM service most convenient, there were nevertheless some technical issues that arose during the study. For example, one participant found that messages were not being transmitted and so an alternative IM software package was used following email discussion between both parties. As well as losing time, it was felt the incident had fractured the flow of the interview. Additionally, one participant reported that the amount of text that could be transferred in one message was limited and that perplexed them.

4. The researchers noted the absence of body language, such as posture or facial expressions, and vocal qualities, such as volume, speed or tone. However, the use of abbreviations and emoticons was common within the interviews and the researchers reflected on their limited understanding of these at the time and how a clearer insight into their use would have helped in the flow and interaction with participants. The researchers note the challenges of ascertaining whether a participant was upset or uncomfortable with any aspect of the interview questions.

5. Unlike the face-to-face interview that can use non-verbal communication to convey a sense of attentiveness and demonstrate to the participant that the interviewer is listening, the online interview does not offer such options and the researchers described how they misinterpreted silence. That is, the participant was reflecting on a point made but the researcher thought they were ready for the next question.

the researcher should attempt to communicate on a personal basis and make each person feel valued.

2. *Subject line:* If emailing participants to invite them to participate in the online interview, include clear and succinct information in the subject line (e.g. 'Invitation to participate in research study'). This may help prevent potential participants from deleting the email without it being read.

3. *Explain the research clearly:* Researchers should explain the nature and purpose of the research as explicitly as possible but in lay terms.

It is important that potential participants are made fully aware of what the project is about, not least to be able to make an informed choice about whether to volunteer or not. Beyond this, being clear and open may foster a sense of transparency and trust and this is especially important when conducting research online. Be clear about what is being asked of each participant, how much time is being requested, how will they participate, how many questions will be asked, how many times will they be contacted, what will happen with their responses and so on. As well as being good practice and likely to impact on participation and retention, such explicit briefing is required by ethics committees.

4. *Ethical considerations:* Participants may have more concerns about their anonymity as well as confidentiality of their textual responses and so researchers must provide clear and accessible information about these issues. It is good practice to include details of the ethics committee responsible for approving the research study as well as details on how participants can contact researchers before, during and after a study. Be clear and upfront about any potential risks that may harm participants and provide contact details for relevant support services, should they become upset as a result of the interview.

5. *Interview questions:* Researchers need to consider carefully the questions that they wish to ask (see Box 2.3, Developing online interview questions). Regardless of whether the interview is taking place via email or IM, researchers should explore with participants their needs with regards processing questions and responding to them. For example, as Jowett *et al.* (2011) report, based on their observations they offered participants the opportunity to undertake the interview via IM over a number of sessions, or in a single session but with regular breaks. Consider also the sequence of questions and the transition from specific to more abstract questions over the course of the interview, as you would do for a face-to-face interview. Preparing a short summary of responses periodically and feeding that back to the participant can be a good way not only to convey a sense that the researcher is engaged and attentive but also to check for accuracy, interpretation and completeness.

6. *Deadlines and timelines:* Participants should be made clear as to the deadlines for responding to questions (e.g. email interviews) but these should be reasonable in the context of their everyday lives. Researchers should be mindful of other factors or reasons as to why participants may not be able to respond promptly. This timeline may be something negotiated with participants at the outset of the online interview

and revisited if required. Similarly, for interviews conducted via IM, researchers should attempt to schedule session(s) at a convenient time for the participant. Moreover, these sessions may be of varying duration and so time demands and associated fatigue should always be considered and actions taken accordingly to facilitate the process.

7. *Data quality:* Great care should be given to engaging participants throughout the online interview in order to produce sufficient data and of good quality. A motivated and engaged participant can yield considerable rich data for research purposes. Many of the activities suggested thus far may help contribute to a successful online interview (e.g. self-disclosure).

BOX 2.3 Developing online interview questions

An essential component of the online interview is the actual questions that are developed. The process is no different for face-to-face interviews but researchers should keep in mind the fact that the interview is taking place online and therefore particular attention should be given to the clarity of questions. Here are some useful reminders on how best to develop interview questions, together with some examples.

1. Ask questions that are likely to generate the most information about the phenomenon being studied.
   Example: Could you tell me what first interested you in studying psychology?

2. The best interview questions are those that are open-ended and cannot simply be answered by a simple 'Yes' or 'No'.
   Example: What do you find to be the most challenging parts of your psychology degree course? Can you explain what it is you find challenging about them?

3. All questions should be easy to understand, neutral and sensitive to the individual being interviewed. In order to achieve this, researchers should pilot their interview questions using participants similar to those who will ultimately be part of the actual study. Feedback should be invited by respondents about how easy questions were to answer. Researchers should note and amend any questions that respondents felt were problematic, for whatever reason.

4. Interviews should begin with more general, easier questions before moving on to more specific or difficult questions. This can help the interviewee not only feel more confident but also generate richer responses and yield more helpful and insightful data.

Chapter summary

As we have seen throughout this chapter, there are a number of useful possibilities with regards effective online interviewing. However, researchers have important decisions to make, particularly in terms of whether to conduct them using an asynchronous or synchronous format. Each has its own strengths and weaknesses but can provide a participant-friendly means through which to gain a rich set of data. Regardless of which type of online interview is ultimately selected, there are some useful guidelines and suggestions that researchers should bear in mind while undertaking such online qualitative interviews.

Further reading

Ayling, R. & Mewse, A.J. (2009). Evaluating Internet interviews with gay men. *Qualitative Health Research*, 19, 566–576.

Egan, J., Chenoweth, L. & McAuliffe, D. (2006). Email-facilitated qualitative interviews with traumatic brain injury survivors: a new and accessible method. *Brain Injury*, 20(12), 1283–1294.

Jowett, A., Peel, E. & Shaw, R. (2011). Online interviewing in psychology: reflections on the process. *Qualitative Research in Psychology*, 8(4), 354–369.

Hinchcliffe, V. & Gavin, H. (2009). Social and virtual networks: evaluating synchronous online interviewing using instant messenger. *The Qualitative Report*, 14(2), 318–340.

Hunt, N. & McHale, S. (2007). A practical guide to the e-mail interview. *Qualitative Health Research*, 17, 1415–1421.

Paterson, B. & Scott-Findley, S. (2002). Critical issues in interviewing people with traumatic brain injury. *Qualitative Health Research*, 12, 399–409.

CHAPTER 3

Online Focus Groups

This chapter begins by providing a brief definition of the traditional face-to-face focus group and identifying the key features of this research tool as well as potentially problematic features. Following this, the online focus group is introduced and a number of potential benefits as well as challenges are discussed. Next, the chapter describes the difference between asynchronous and synchronous communication and the two main types of online focus group based on this distinction. From here, the chapter continues with two types of asynchronous online focus, namely those using a discussion forum format and those using an email distribution list. The particular features of these two types of asynchronous online focus groups are described as well as strategies that may help promote successful engagement by group participants. Attention is then turned to exploring various synchronous online focus groups, including chat rooms, virtual reality and voice and video platforms. The nature of online communication within the focus group scenario as well as the selected design issues that researchers must consider are discussed. In addition, issues facing the researcher through the online environment, technology, participants as well as the focus group moderation are identified and discussed.

Face-to-face focus groups

A focus group is a 'carefully planned discussion designed to obtain perceptions on a defined area of interest in a permissive, non-threatening environment' (Krueger, 1994, p. 6). While a number of definitions have been proposed over the years (e.g. Merton, 1987), most researchers consider focus groups as a means of exploiting group interaction in order to explore a particular topic of interest.

Indeed, the face-to-face focus group has been one of the most popular qualitative research tools across a range of disciplines and the field of psychology is no exception.

In essence, the face-to-face focus group comprises a limited number of participants, often between 6 and 10, who have been invited on the basis of some predetermined attribute or set of attributes (e.g. senior manager, smoker, adolescent, football supporter) to come together to discuss a specific topic, usually with a moderator who has a prepared list of discussion topics or questions.

As each group begins to discuss the particular topic, each member will become increasingly aware of the views and opinions of other members of the group. An individual group member may then try to explain and defend their own position and in doing so, the group enters into a 'negotiation process'. This means that the data collected during a face-to-face focus group is a consequence of the interpersonal interactions and exchanges that have taken place rather than simply an individual expressing their single viewpoint. It is fair to say that this dynamic process has been regarded as probably the most distinctive feature of this method but there has been much criticism levelled at this approach.

The main criticisms of the focus group method arise from the fact that the group members are all temporally and spatially co-present. Simply put, they interact face-to-face with each other at the same time. Consequently, it has been argued that this co-presence heightens social desirability and group norms and can often lead to inhibition and passive agreement with the group position. In short, it is not possible to determine whether the opinions expressed during the face-to-face focus group discussion have arisen from what each individual participant has to say or from 'conformance or censoring, coercion, conflict avoidance or just plain fickleness' (Duggleby, 2000, p. 294).

Despite these criticisms, focus groups have gained academic credibility over the years as researchers have become increasingly familiar and experienced in managing the interaction between group participants. Indeed, this interaction has allowed many psychologists to obtain a rich understanding of the thinking, language and social reality of participants' experiences by eliciting the responses that emerge from the group dynamics, discussions, interactions and reactions.

Online focus groups

An online focus group can be defined as 'a selected group of individuals who have volunteered to participate in a moderated, structured, online discussion in order to explore a particular topic for the purpose of research' (Peacock *et al.*, 2009, p. 119). Indeed, since the advent of the Internet and technological advances that have occurred since then, researchers wishing to engage in online focus groups have several options available to them (see Section 'Types of online focus groups'). Broadly speaking, online focus groups can be either asynchronous or synchronous and within each of these categories, there exists a number of possibilities as to how the online focus group can operate. However, while there has been a growth in the number of psychological research studies that have employed an online focus group method, there is still much confusion and debate within the field. For example, there is still debate as to what an online focus group actually is, how many people should participate, how long should the online focus group last, what technology (i.e. type of internet-mediated communication) should be used, what type of participant should be invited, what style of moderation should be undertaken and so on. With this in mind, this chapter seeks to provide an overview of some of these issues and offer helpful suggestions to those new to online focus groups and thinking about using them for psychological research. As with other online methods, there is no right or wrong answer but rather a number of issues that each individual researcher needs to consider as well as factoring in issues of resource (i.e. finance and time) and technological expertise. Throughout this chapter, we shall discuss some of these issues in an effort to help the researcher get the most from their online focus group experience.

Potential benefits of online focus groups

There are several potential benefits that may arise when using online focus groups to research psychological phenomenon.

Cost

In comparison to traditional face-to-face groups, the costs of running an online focus group may be less. For example, traditional face-to-face groups usually incur costs relating to the venue, audiotaping (or videotaping in some studies) and transcription of the data. For online focus groups, these costs may not be relevant; however, it does not infer that there are no costs involved. The researcher still needs to consider any costs attached to the software used to facilitate the study. In some instances, such as an asynchronous online focus group using a discussion forum, there may be freely available software that meets the needs of the study (see Section 'Online software packages'). For other studies, a subscription to a website or company offering specific software may need to be purchased for the duration of the project. However, it is generally felt that the online focus group can be a less expensive means through which to collect data than its face-to-face equivalent. Several researchers have argued that the online focus group is a viable, if not preferable, alternative to the traditional face-to-face focus group (Turney & Pocknee, 2005; Watson *et al.*, 2006). Indeed, in a discussion of the practical benefits of the online focus group, Murray (1997) concluded 'The use of VFGs [virtual focus groups] has provided valuable research data that could have not been readily obtained using other methods and from participants whom I could not have otherwise hoped to gather together for discussions without considerable expense' (p. 548).

Timing and location

Conducting an online focus group could help eliminate the (often) difficult challenges associated with face-to-face groups in relation to timing and geography. For example, participants in an online focus group simply have to log on at a pre-arranged time and could do so from any convenient location (e.g. home or work). For face-to-face focus groups, there may be difficulties surrounding participants' ability to travel to and engage in the focus group. Furthermore, there may be other reasons as to why participants may not be able to physically attend a focus group (e.g. disability, childcare, shift work) and therefore, an online focus group may be an attractive solution. In addition, online focus groups may be especially helpful in the context of cross-cultural research where participants may be located in different countries or even continents. However, the researcher must be mindful of coordinating participation from individuals in different time zones, which is not always an easy task.

Accessing hard to reach populations

Online focus groups may be beneficial to researchers because they can potentially engage individuals who might otherwise have been difficult to reach. There may be several reasons as to why certain individuals are difficult to engage in psychological research. For example, they may live in remote areas and therefore, the chances of engaging in a face-to-face focus group would be negligible. Alternatively, a participant may hold extreme or non-traditional views on a controversial topic and may feel they can only be expressed safely within the online setting. In addition, there may be health-related reasons as to why the target population may be hard to reach (see Box 3.1, Example of an asynchronous online focus group).

Size of the group

In theory, the online focus group can be as large or small as you wish and may include several dozen members or as few as 3 or 4. An important point to note is that the online focus group is not constrained in the same way as a face-to-face group but the researcher must still be mindful of having too few or too many group participants.

Anonymity

By hosting a focus group online, there is the opportunity for participants to engage with the process but still remain anonymous. Apart from any registration procedures and personal details given that only the moderator or the researcher may see, the only public information seen by others may simply be a username. As a result, some participants may feel better able to contribute to the research study. Furthermore, by remaining anonymous, some participants may feel more able to discuss more sensitive, personal or stigmatized topics. Indeed, Suzuki & Calvo (2004) have endorsed this sentiment and argued that the perceived anonymity conferred online may be especially helpful to young people and may allow them to explore sensitive issues or topics that they may feel unable to do so with family, friends or other adults and to experiment with personal communication styles that might not be salient in face-to-face interaction. This is a result of the

BOX 3.1   Example of asynchronous online focus group

Summary of research from Tates *et al.* (2009). Online focus groups as a tool to collect data in hard-to-include populations: examples from paediatric oncology. *BMC Medical Research Methodology*, 9 (15).

Background

This study conducted a series of asynchronous online focus groups using discussion forums with children in active treatment for paediatric cancer, their parents and child survivors of paediatric cancer separately, to determine what constitutes good quality of communication in terms of participation and role delineation from their point of view.

Rationale for asynchronous online focus group

The authors of this study reviewed and considered the potential benefits of using an online focus group methodology and noted the resource and cost efficiencies offered. However, the main consideration focussed on the challenge of engaging children living with cancer and their parents in research. It was viewed as unlikely that a traditional face-to-face format would be manageable and be convenient to participants. Therefore, the authors considered the online focus group to be more practical, given the considerable challenges faced by the children and their families. In addition, they considered the Internet to be something that was familiar to children and therefore represented a viable research data collection tool. The specific choice of asynchronous discussion forum was made in order to further accommodate the needs of participants and their illness.

The experience of running the online focus groups

The authors reported that the online focus groups yielded rich and detailed qualitative data. However, they also evaluated the experience of participating in the asynchronous online focus group from the perspective of the children and parents and reported their findings and participant reflections.

First, the authors noted that the children in active treatment, their parents as well as other paediatric cancer survivors were able to engage with the online discussion during the weeklong session. Second, they noted that the group dynamics varied across the three online focus groups. The youngest age group appeared to direct their online comments to the moderator as opposed to others in the group. It was noted that the children answered all the questions and follow up probes. In the group that included adolescents, a more interactive style of online communication was reported. In contrast, the interaction in the parents group was deemed to be far less successful though the study authors did note that all answers were carefully considered and detailed. Indeed, the parents commented, 'It was not really a group discussion, more like answers to statements'.

Second, the participants provided feedback through a questionnaire after the focus group ended. Ease of use of the online group discussion board was considered to be good by the majority of the participants (24 of 31 respondents), just as most group participants positively valued the frequency of one question a day (24 of 31 respondents). In the study, a time period of 1 week for joining the group discussion was set. All the participants in the patient group reported being satisfied with this time frame, whereas most survivors and parents would have preferred an extended duration.

Interestingly, the authors asked if the participants would have participated in a face-to-face focus group. The responses revealed that 11 participants responded positively (1 patient, 4 parents, 6 survivors), 11 participants replied that they would not have joined a traditional group discussion (6 parents, 5 survivors), and 9 participants were not sure (3 patients, 1 parent, 5 survivors). When participants were asked which mode of group discussion they would have preferred to join if they had been free to choose any, 22 of 31 participants chose the online discussion (3 patients, 9 parents, 10 survivors).

The evaluation conducted by the authors also highlighted that most respondents had clear and outspoken ideas about the relative advantages and drawbacks of online focus group discussions. Participants who would have preferred a face-to-face group considered the online mode of discussion less personal. A strong and consistent finding reported by the authors that emerged in each group, was the advantage of participant convenience attributed to online communication. Most participants expressed great comfort with the flexibility of logging in at their own pace and time.

A particular feature, strongly endorsed by the group participants, was the anonymity conferred by the online platform used. Specifically, they felt more at ease and comfortable with regards expressing their views and felt the anonymity offered via the online discussion tool contributed to their self-disclosure: 'It is sometimes difficult thinking about hard times you have had in the past. With strangers it is even more difficult to find the right words. On the Internet it is easier to be yourself' (survivor).

Overall, the authors reflect on their research and concluded that the online environment allowed participants to discuss personal issues in ways that might not have been witnessed offline.

'online dis-inhibition' effect (Suler, 2004) that argues that people online can act or behave in ways that they would not necessarily do in a face-to-face interaction. However, this can be a double-edged sword as the conferred anonymity may lead to more negative interactions (see Section 'Potential challenges of online focus groups').

Reduction in unequal power relationships

In the context of an online focus group, the researcher and the participants are not physically in the presence of each other as a consequence this may serve to reduce unequal power relations. In particular, power relations that may have existed as a result of age, gender, and ethnicity in a traditional face-to-face focus group may not be as problematic and as such participant engagement may be facilitated. Indeed, as Kitchin (1998) has suggested, the Internet and associated technologies are 'creating new social spaces that lack the formal qualities of geographic spaces' (p. 386). That is, the Internet may offer the potential to facilitate research situations that challenge some of the typical power relationships witnessed in traditional methodologies and the online focus group is a prime example. As a result, participants who may not have felt confident to engage in a face-to-face focus group may do so with more ease and comfort. Indeed, one of the concerns of early researchers using online methods was that group participants would not be able to develop rapport with the researcher or relationships with each other. However, a growing body of literature has since demonstrated that even in the absence of visual or aural cues that normally influence personal impressions, individuals are able to develop close relationships with one another, and often more quickly than in offline settings. As Fox *et al.* (2007) note 'I was struck by the participants' confidence when meeting both me and a group of unfamiliar others. This confidence might have been linked to a variety of factors, including their familiarity with, or enjoyment of, engaging in synchronous chat; a heightened sense of anonymity; and the convenience of taking part from home' (p. 545).

Digital record

If a text-based online focus group format is used, then there is a digital record of the discussion among group participants. This means that the researcher does not need to transcribe the group discussion verbatim, thus, saving valuable time and resource as well as the challenge of trying to identify who said what. The fact that there exists a digital record of the focus group interaction immediately also allows the researcher to begin analysis of the transcript straight away. This may be helpful in terms of recalling important information about the focus group and may facilitate the interpretation of the data through the ability of the researcher to remember important contextual information.

Potential challenges of online focus groups

Online focus groups do have their challenges and the researcher needs to be mindful of these as they design and conduct their study. While there are several potential limitations revolving around access to the Internet, technological expertise and digital literacy (see Chapter 1), there are several issues that are, perhaps, more salient in the context of an online focus group. These will now be described.

Drop out

One of the most difficult challenges facing the researcher who wishes to use the online focus group method is that of drop out. However, it is fair to say that the potential significance of this problem may vary depending on the specific type (i.e. asynchronous or synchronous) of group chosen, the skills of the moderator as well as background characteristics and level of motivation of the participants themselves. Drop out may take place even before any discussion has occurred as a participant may fail to log on and participate even after having agreed to do so. Similarly, drop out may occur once the research is up and running and group members may either 'disappear' or be non-responsive to contact from the researcher or moderator or actively withdraw from the study (Box 3.2, Strategies for encouraging participation in asynchronous online focus groups).

Non-verbal information (text-based groups only)

In a face-to-face context, focus group participants will provide a large amount of non-verbal information that the moderator can potentially use as part of their quest to explore a particular topic. For example, a member may be sharing their views about a controversial topic, or a topic they feel especially passionate about and their facial or body language may be important to observe. In the online focus group format, the primary means of communication is through text; therefore, this important non-verbal information will be lost. However, with an increasing number of people now texting via mobile phones and communicating online (e.g. twitter), it is possible that some limited information can be conveyed through the use of emoticons or text speak (e.g. lol = laugh out loud). However, this is likely to be dependent on the particular experience and background of the individuals participating in the online group.

BOX 3.2   Strategies for encouraging participation in asynchronous online focus groups

According to van Patten (2011), there are several simple strategies that the researcher can employ to facilitate and sustain focus group participation in the asynchronous online setting.

1. Selecting your participants

It is more than likely that participants who are interested in a particular topic will have more to say on the subject and may be more active in an asynchronous online focus group discussion. Therefore, the researcher should think carefully about who they wish to participate in their online focus group, for example, a broad spectrum reflecting different levels of interest in a topic or participants who all share a keen interest in the topic of the research or a mixture of both.

2. Offering the right incentive

Depending on the resources available to the researcher, the use of incentives may be considered as a strategy to engage participants. Assuming that an incentive can be offered, the researcher needs to carefully consider which type of incentive may be the best. For example, young people may wish to receive an iTunes voucher as a 'thank you' gift, while older participants may appreciate a general shopping or restaurant voucher. Alternatively, the researcher may wish to offer a choice of vouchers and simply ask participants to choose which they would prefer. As a result of the online nature of the research, researchers may find it preferable to use an e-voucher as opposed to posting a gift card to the participant. This often allows the researcher more reassurance that the participant has received the incentive. Group participants may also prefer not to disclose their home address during the research process. It is also worth noting that sometimes participants have a vested interest in the research and may participate willingly on condition that they receive an executive summary of the study, outlining the key findings.

3. Manage expectations early

It is important to work with participants early to ensure that their expectations surrounding the online focus group are managed appropriately.

This will involve spelling it out clearly what will be involved in the research and what is expected of them. This may be done via the original recruitment activity that first engaged the participant in the study (e.g. mail shot, online advert) but researchers may also wish to remind participants at the start of the actual focus group about what is expected and how much time and effort is required.

4. Limit the number of questions

There is sometimes a temptation to ask too many questions and this can have a negative impact on participant engagement so the researcher needs to carefully consider how many questions are absolutely essential. For participants, it takes time to log in to the group, read any questions and/or comments posted and to formulate and post their reply. It is very easy to underestimate how much time this can take and participants may grow tired or bored of the process quickly. Researchers may wish to consider telling participants at the outset how many questions they will be asked.

5. Do something to make it more visually appealing

Asynchronous discussion forums can often look a little text heavy and to the participant this may be seen as something dull and boring. It is important to try and make your discussion forum as attractive as possible. This can be done in a range of ways including, different colours and images or links on the site. The researcher may also wish to upload a picture of them on to the forum.

6. Work at it

Even if the group of participants selected to engage with the online focus group have an interest in the topic, engagement is not a given and the researcher still needs to work hard to create and sustain engagement. Interacting with participants early on in the process can do this. Responding to the required participation can help and ensure that participants are made to feel welcome as they join the group.

7. Make it a conversation

In the absence of traditional rapport building strategies, the researcher or moderator needs to rely on the text to engage participants. A simple way to do this is to keep things chatty and light early on and be personal in replies. Using words such as 'seeing' and 'hearing' can be used to echo the face-to-face discussion. Similarly, using the term 'I' instead of 'we' can be seen as less impersonal.

8. Use of a variety of approaches
Depending on the nature of the research and duration of the focus group, it is suggested that varying the activities or types of questions can be a good thing to keep participants engaged. Moreover, if the study is expected to last several days, then it might be worth considering a 'rest' day where no new questions are posted and participants are told this so they have a chance to catch up on the unfolding conversation(s).

9. Reward desired behaviour
It is important to set the ground rules at the start of the focus group and comment positively on the behaviour that you'd like to see by participants and this could be done by a simple 'thank you' for example.

10. Use the moderator tools available
There is usually a range of tools available to the moderator and these can be used to encourage and sustain engagement. For example, sending emails to group members to remind them to participate or to selected individuals might be considered. While online platforms may vary in the functions offered, the majority can tell you who has logged in and how active they have been in the focus group discussion. This may prove to be a useful tool to use in order to monitor the development of the group over time.

Vocal cues (text-based groups only)

In addition to the absence of non-verbal cues, moderators will also not be able to pick up on any vocal cues that might have been present face-to-face. For example, participants may use inflections and intonation to make a particular statement stand out or to add emphasis to a point.

Group dynamics

During the course of an online focus group, there is a danger that some participants may use offensive or inflammatory remarks as a result of the anonymity conferred by the internet-mediated nature of the communication. This may be the result of the 'online dis-inhibition' effect (Suler, 2004) that has been noted previously. As a result, there might be potential conflict between members of the group.

Similarly, even within online groups, there is the potential for 2 or 3 members to engage only with each other and form cliques. The longer the online group the greater the likelihood but this can be easily managed by a skilled moderator who can draw everyone into the discussion should this happen.

Types of online focus groups

Broadly speaking, there are two main types of online focus groups: asynchronous and synchronous. The key difference between these two types rests on whether the online group discussion between participants is in real-time (synchronous) or not (asynchronous). Choosing between these two types may be relatively easy, depending on the nature of the research study or it may be more complex. It should be noted, however, that the difference between them may be an important one. Previous studies have suggested that the discussions which take place may differ, depending on whether the focus group members are temporally co-present or not.

In the next two sections, we shall consider each of these two broad types of online focus groups. In addition, we shall discuss the various communication tools that could be employed to undertake these types of online focus group.

Asynchronous online focus groups

Asynchronous online focus groups bring group participants together over the course of a defined period of time (e.g. a week or a month). As such, the group members need not be online at the same time but rather they access and participate in the online focus group discussion at a time convenient to them. As a result of this, a key advantage is that group participants are not under any time pressure to respond to a particular question or comment, but rather they can potentially write a more detailed and considered response (Mann & Stewart, 2000; Murray, 2004). According to Joinson (2003), 'once the pressure to reply immediately is removed, the person has the opportunity to move scarce cognitive resources from the management of the conversation to the actual message' (p. 22). Indeed, it may be that such benefits to participants are most likely felt when personal or sensitive discussions are taking place (e.g. traumatic experiences, bullying, illness). Participants will have control over what they feel comfortable revealing. However, asynchronous communication is not without its potential limitations as some authors have argued that spontaneity in the discussion is perhaps limited (Oringderff, 2004). Researchers should, therefore, reflect on how important these issues are in the context of their own study.

The benefits of such asynchronous communication are not exclusive to participants; rather, researchers may also find the absence of time pressure to be helpful. For example, there may be more time available to researchers to consider and reflect upon the responses and comments made by group participants. This may be something that is helpful to researchers in terms of shaping or amending subsequent questions to be used in the group discussion. Similarly, it may provide greater opportunity for researchers to check the participants' meanings and to ensure that the experiences being discussed are fully understood and interpreted correctly. In essence, researchers can begin to reflect on the data being generated and this will undoubtedly be helpful when it comes to later analysis and write up, and as Williams *et al.* (2012) argue, asynchronous communication 'increases opportunities for moving iteratively between data collection and data interpretation throughout the research process and allows for rich, robust, qualitative findings' (p. 375).

There are two popular types of asynchronous text-based communication that have proven popular in psychological research – discussion forums and email distribution lists.

Discussion forums

Discussion forums (also known as bulletin or message boards or Internet forums) are accessed via websites and provide group participants the opportunity to engage in conversation using a tree-like structure. That is to say, different topics or issues may be discussed within sub-sections. Within each of these different sections or sub-sections, group participants can initiate their own discussion (known as a 'conversation thread') or they can respond to a conversation thread already present. Messages posted to discussion forums are known as 'posts' or 'postings' and can be read by everyone who has access to the discussion forum being used for the research study (see Table 3.1, 'Example structure of an online discussion forum').

In terms of access to discussion forums, some websites require the user to register before they can read or contribute to discussions while others do not. The researcher may wish to consider these options carefully since some argue (e.g. Prandy *et al.*, 2001) that discussion forums requiring registration have a number of strengths, especially in relation to the issues of group participant identification. By having participants register, the researcher is able to have more control over the group composition as well as being able to obtain relevant background information. For group participants, being registered means that all they now have to do is choose a username (e.g. mickeymouse123). By having only their username visible to the other focus group participants, an individual may feel more comfortable that their real name, or other personal information, is not seen.

Table 3.1 Example structure of online discussion forum

General	Threads/Posts	Last post
Introduce yourself to others in the group	6/24	6.7.15 19.13 p.m.
About the researcher	1/7	5.7.15 15.49 p.m.
About the research		
What is this research about?	4/14	9.7.15 08.06 a.m.
Why discuss things online?	2/3	8.7.15 17.56 p.m.
What is expected of me?	1/9	8.7.15 13.13 p.m.
The questions to discuss		
What do you think about immigration to the UK?	1/24	16.7.15 23.08 p.m.
How have you been personally affected?	1/4	18.7.15 12.11 p.m.

For group participants, the use of an online discussion board may be something familiar but for others it may be more confusing. The researcher needs to be aware of participant experience and familiarity with this type of Internet-mediated communication. Similarly, for the moderator of the online focus group who uses a discussion board format, there may be challenges in terms of technical expertise required; however, with a growing number of websites offering ready-made discussion forums, this problem should not be insurmountable (see Section 'Online software packages').

A potentially serious problem when undertaking asynchronous online focus groups is that of participant non-engagement. As noted previously, there is no agreed time or (online) space which has been set aside for the focus group but rather it rests on the shoulders of the participant to take time out of their daily lives to log on to read and respond to messages posted to the group. It is incredibly easy for a participant within an asynchronous group discussion to disengage and stop reading and responding to messages. The moderator of such a group has a very important role in trying to engage all participants in the online discussion process and to sustain that engagement. For this particular type of online focus group, active moderation is essential or else the text-based environment may not lend itself to a stimulating and fulfilling discussion. Therefore, some advocate that a small focus group is better with 5–6 participants as opposed to something much larger and arguably more difficult to moderate properly. In larger groups, it becomes even easier for a participant to fall off the moderator's radar.

Email distribution lists

Using an email distribution list to run an online focus group is likely to use a single central email address to which all messages are sent before being forwarded to the list of recipients. For some researchers, the decision to use an email distribution list may be grounded in the fact that many people are familiar with emails and may feel more comfortable using them to convey their views or opinion on a specific topic. While an email is perhaps less visually appealing than a discussion forum, it does offer similar levels of control to the researcher. For example, the researcher has control over who is on the distribution list and who has access to information about the discussion and its recipients. Similarly, the researcher is able to filter the email discussions and if they wish, send them as a digest at regular intervals (e.g. daily or weekly). Such email distribution lists can be moderated with contributions edited to remove any header or footer information or perhaps to insert comments and/ or questions or probes to focus participants on a specific issue. Over time, however, this particular means of collecting data has become less popular and indeed some researchers view research through email lists as more akin to a group interview rather than a true focus group technique (Di Fraia, 2004).

Synchronous online focus groups

Synchronous online focus groups have many similarities when compared with traditional face-to-face focus groups in that they occur in real time, usually at a pre-arranged time (e.g. 7 p.m. GMT). Participants react and respond to the comments made by other members as they are received. The online conversations are more akin to a face-to-face conversation and the online discussion may be fast paced and even chaotic at times.

There is considerable variation in the types of synchronous communication that may be used for online focus groups. Three types of synchronous online focus groups will now be described– text-based, virtual reality and voice/video.

Text-based chat rooms

Chat rooms are the most common type of synchronous format used to run an online focus group. Here, members of an online focus group would be logged on to the Internet simultaneously and interact with each other in a similar way to a face-to-face exchange, responding to questions posed by the moderator as well as responding to comments made by other participants. It should be noted that like discussion forums, using a chat room also offers the same opportunities for participants in terms of registration and the use of a username (Box 3.3).

Text-based virtual reality

An alternative form of synchronous online focus group may be conducted using Networked Virtual Reality or Graphical MUDs.

BOX 3.3　Example of synchronous online focus group using a chat room

Summary of research from Fox *et al.* (2007). Doing synchronous online focus groups with young people: methodological reflections. *Qualitative Health Research*, 17(4), 539–547.

Background

This study aimed to examine the appearance-related concerns of young people who were living with a long-term skin condition. Its aims were to generate a rich and in-depth account of the breadth and diversity of individual experiences. It had been noted that in previous research, there was a preference for quantifying experience but little attempt had been made to ask young people directly about their own experiences, thoughts, feelings and concerns.

Rationale for synchronous online focus group

The authors of this study cite a number of factors that may rule out the use of face-to-face focus groups, including personal organization, access to transport as well as the confidence required to meet strangers in an unfamiliar location. Indeed, it was the fact that the young people had a visible difference that led the authors to conclude that an online focus group may represent a more acceptable alternative. Furthermore, as young people are more likely to be Internet savvy and engage with it across several areas of their daily lives (e.g. home, school, entertainment) it was concluded that an online approach would be appropriate. Moreover, given the fact that the young people were likely to be familiar with fast moving, online conversations through social networking, texting and instant messaging, it was felt that a synchronous format would be most applicable. However, the authors did note researcher-participant dynamics as a further factor that might be more problematic if done face-to-face.

The experience of running online focus groups

The process of establishing the online environment was a challenging one and the authors note a number of issues, not least getting a date and time to suit the group of young people participating in the discussions. With participants drawn from different time zones it was decided to run separate groups for those in the United Kingdom and those outside. Considerable care was also taken to convey a friendly, inviting and supportive online environment; this included a welcome page where group participants could wait between logging in and actually beginning the discussion. This page offered a venue through which the authors could reiterate the aims of the group discussion as well as articulate the expectations with regards group conduct and behaviour as well as encouraging active contribution.

The lead author (Fox) was also the moderator for the online focus groups and she notes the challenge of being a moderator and keeping up to speed with the unfolding online interactions among participants. The importance of experience is emphasized and through pilot work, she was able to gain more familiarity and confidence with online technology and demands of the situation. In addition, the number of participants was important for the speed and complexity of the online conversation but she notes a 50% drop out rate for some sessions. Conversely, the absence of any contribution from participants was also viewed as challenging in that silence could be seen as a lack of engagement but it could also mean that participants were thinking about an issue before deciding what to say and posting a message. Similar to face-to-face groups, the author also reports having to refocus the group from time to time back to the core issue.

In this scenario, the online focus group is undertaken that not only allows participants to communicate via text but also to have a graphical representation (e.g. avatar). Indeed, in some platforms, there is also a graphical representation of the world (e.g. Second Life). Platforms such as Second Life allow an individual to design and customize their own online avatar. These avatars are, in essence, a virtual representation of the person sat behind the computer screen and in the context of a focus group, are its members. In this scenario, focus group participants are part of a 3D world, in which they can move about or interact with other focus group participants. Researchers wishing to explore this virtual venue for their research can also design and customize their own online setting (e.g. a research laboratory or simply a room with sofas). Once an appropriate virtual venue has been designed and participants have been recruited, the focus group can commence and this is typically through text-based discussion that will appear either at the side or the bottom of the screen. Therefore, for researchers wishing to conduct an online focus group, this combination of text and virtual reality offers an altogether different type of experience for participants.

The potential benefits from this type of blended text-virtual reality platform may be particularly located in the increased sense of 'being somewhere' and that the focus group participants are coexisting both physically and textually. The hope is that such an environment will serve to facilitate and encourage a greater depth of interaction and discussion between the online focus group members. Indeed, according to Schroeder (1997), 'the combined effect of using text, navigating in a 3-D environment and engaging with others via avatars ... is greater than the sum of its parts' (p. 7). Furthermore, it is hoped that concerns about online focus groups, such as lack of visible cues, that have limited the interpretation and analysis of data may be addressed to some extent. For example, some avatars are able to display facial expressions and this can aid the focus group moderator in terms of gauging the reactions and feelings of participants to specific points or issues.

A final point as echoed in the work of Williams (2003) is that even in such virtual environments, researchers do need to consider the venue in which the online focus group will take place. As noted earlier, it is possible to customize the setting and attention should be given to ensure that the venue is appropriate and fit for purpose. The decisions made by Williams (2003) in his research, using such virtual environments, illustrate some of the choices available to researchers. For example, it was decided that the venue should be a private one and that the online focus group moderator and the participants should be present. In addition, the venue for the online focus group within the virtual environment should be free from surveillance as many such environments have monitors that it was felt may impact upon the group discussion.

A quiet venue was selected, in as much as it was away from the many distractions contained within such environments, such as malls or gambling venues. Finally, he ensured that the venue was warm, friendly and most of all, welcoming.

Voice and video platforms

There are a number of synchronous platforms that allow for both voice and video chat and are most akin to the look and feel of a traditional face-to-face focus group. A growing number of online environments are equipped with voice over IP (VoIP) that may assist the researcher in conducting a blended text, voice and video discussion. A common example of such a platform is Skype that has in excess of 663 million users, and has been providing a low cost platform for users since 2003 (see Box 3.4, Using Skype for focus group research).

BOX 3.4 Using Skype for focus group research

In an evaluation of Skype as a potential synchronous platform to undertake focus group research, a team (Sintjago & Link, 2012) of qualitative researchers based in North America undertook an analysis of its potential through simulated focus groups and noted the following strengths and weaknesses:

- A low cost or free chat platform
- Moderation problems since it is structured to operate as a tool to aid communication between peers, as opposed to a more structured conversation with a moderator present
- Privacy settings not always transparent
- Offers a range of communication modes including voice, video and file share though this requires more bandwith and may pose a problem for some individuals with limited Internet access.

The team of researchers concluded that 'With good bandwith, however, along with a good moderator introduction to set participants at ease, clear details on how communication will take place through Skype, and a good set of questions, Skype can be a useful tool for synchronous online focus groups'.

The nature of online communication

In the previous section, we considered both asynchronous and synchronous types of online focus groups and explored some of their advantages and disadvantages. However, with the exception of voice or video platforms, text-based communication is at the heart of this process and researchers may well reflect on the impact of computer-mediated communication on the ability of participants to capture personal beliefs, attitudes and life experiences. Whereas in asynchronous platforms, the pressure to read and reply instantly is absent the opposite is true for synchronous online focus groups. In this latter scenario, the ability of the participant to consider their reply and type a response quickly is crucial.

In addition, researchers may well be concerned about the nature of the online communication and ask themselves whether such text-based interaction between participants is helpful. Researchers should not worry as online communication (just like offline) can present a range of linguistic features that can help capture important aspects of the individual and the social context in which they are presenting aspects of themselves (Williams *et al.*, 2012).

Online communication can employ a range of informal representations of written language such as phonetic spellings and abbreviations, (e.g. where r u? LMAO) as well as more formal features, such as the ability to edit an online comment before posting it (see Table 3.2). Indeed, James & Busher (2009) argue that the combination of written language with conversational aspects of communication, the result is a 'hybrid of both spoken and written language' (p. 107). Furthermore, there are a range of simple, yet effective, conventions that can be used by participants to convey a sense of emotion in their online discussions.

The issue of expression of emotion in the context of online communication is a contentious one. Indeed, Williams *et al.* (2012) note the use of body language and various nonverbal cues in face-to-face communication and how they are largely absent in online communication (i.e. text based). Indeed, some researchers have adopted a somewhat pessimistic and sceptical view of the role of emotion in online communication and have suggested that online communication falls short of 'meaningful discourse' (Mann & Stewart, 2000). In opposition to this, others have suggested that

Table 3.2 Commonly used abbreviations in online communication

AFAIK	As far as I know	IMO	In my opinion
AFK	Away from keyboard	IOW	In other words
BBFN	Bye bye for now	L8R	(See you) later
BG	Big grin	LOL	Laughing out loud
BRB	Be right back	NE1	Anyone
BTW	By the way	NP	No problem
CMIIW	Correct me if I'm wrong	OMG	Oh, my God!
CUL8R	See you later	OTOH	On the other hand
F2F	Face to face (in person)	PM	Private message
FAQ	Frequently asked question	PUTER	Computer
FWIW	For what it is worth	THX	Thanks
FYI	For your information	TMI	Too much information
G2G	I've got to go	TTFN	Ta-ta for now (good-bye)
IC	I see	TY	Thank you
ICWUM	I see what you mean	WB	Welcome back
IM	Instant message	WUF?	Where are you from?

online text-based communication 'should not be underestimated in its capacity to induce strong feelings and reactions' (Watson *et al.*, 2006, p. 552). Certainly, in the context of online discussions among members of health-related online support communities, there is considerable evidence of highly emotive language being used to describe a range of feelings associated with chronic illness, such as despair, pain, loneliness and depression. Indeed, psychologists such as Pennebaker (1993) have suggested that this form of 'expressive' writing can be cathartic for patients and in some instances discussing such personal issues online is preferred to face-to-face discussion (e.g. Buchanan & Coulson, 2007; Malik & Coulson, 2008a).

Designing and running your online focus group

So far in this chapter, we have considered the potential benefits as well as challenges of using an online focus group method for psychological research. In addition, an overview of the various types of online focus group that researchers could use for the purposes of their study has been provided. However, regardless of which type of online focus group selected, there are a number of key research design issues that must be considered carefully.

Number of focus group participants

While the online focus group has, in theory, no upper limit in terms of the number of participants, there is some sense in keeping it 'small'. Indeed, many researchers have opted to retain a sample size for their online focus group that is comparable to that recommended for face-to-face groups. This may well be relevant to those qualitative researchers who wish to gain a rich insight into the experiences of their participants. However, researchers should keep under review the specific aims of their study and what level of interaction may be required. This position has been endorsed by Murray (1997) who typically used between 6 and 8 participants in his studies but stated that 'the off-line group size may not be appropriate in all circumstances, and a large group may be needed to promote the level of discussion and interaction the researcher seeks' (p. 545). That said, a smaller group may be viewed by participants as more intimate and conducive to a group discussion, especially if they are likely to reveal aspects of themselves which they deem personal, sensitive or intimate. In a study by Williams (2009), 21 asynchronous focus groups were reviewed and it was revealed that the mean number of participants was 12. In this review, the sample sizes ranged from 3 group participants (Dickerson & Feitshans, 2003) to 57 participants (Robson, as cited in Stewart & Williams, 2005).

Duration of study

Individual studies will most likely vary in terms of how long their online focus group should be undertaken. In the review by Williams (2009), mentioned previously, asynchronous focus groups ranged in duration from 1 to 24 weeks, with a mean duration of 9 weeks. However, it is noted that only 1 study was located at the upper end (i.e. 24 weeks) and without this study, the average duration is in fact 4 weeks. It is generally felt that 4 weeks is as good a duration as any and may be sufficiently long to conduct the research whilst sustaining the interest of group participants.

The decision as to the duration, of course, is likely to be driven by a range of considerations and researchers should reflect upon the specific research questions underpinning their work, together with how the focus group will be structured and what the topic will be for group discussion. In addition, time and resource issues will also need to be considered. As a result of these deliberations, the number of questions included within the topic guide will vary and this is undoubtedly going to impact upon the duration of the study.

In addition to these issues, Sintjago & Link (2012) identify some useful issues to reflect upon when running the focus group. Let us take a look at each of them.

Online environment

The online environment needs to be an attractive and inviting space that is user friendly. Researchers may wish to upload a short introductory video or mini biography with picture to help participants get to know the moderator, the function and purpose of the group and specific features of the platform. In addition, researchers should implement ways through which group participants can also personalize their online experience, perhaps through a short biography or profile pictures. Above all else the researcher should endeavour to create a warm and welcoming environment. Beyond this, the researcher should try to make it easy for group participants to find things on the site and should not make the site too complex and confusing. A useful rule of thumb is to only include on the site that which is absolutely necessary to undertake the focus group.

Technology issues

Researchers need to be mindful of participants' backgrounds, particularly in terms of technological expertise and familiarity with online communication. Depending on the group of participants, researchers/moderators may wish to find ways they can bring everyone up to speed. This could be done through providing a detailed guide on how to engage successfully with the online group. Alternatively, participants could be asked to try out the various features of the online focus group platform and ask any questions about any aspect of it. Indeed, it is recommended that researchers select platforms and features that participants are likely to be familiar with, however, depending on the nature of the study this may not always be possible. It is also useful to plan for every eventuality and so the researcher may wish to have a number of options available should a participant have a technical problem.

Participants

As noted earlier in this chapter, there may be several reasons as to why it may be advantageous in some instances to keep the number of participants in an online focus group small. For example, it can help reduce the amount of material that a participant has to potentially read if the group is convened using an asynchronous platform (e.g. discussion forum). Moreover, for groups using a synchronous voice/video platform (e.g. Skype) there may be an advantage in terms of problems arising from bandwidth and other data communication problems.

It is advisable to choose an online platform, or way of communicating, that is comfortable and hopefully familiar to the group participants. The researcher should consider early on in the research process factors that may be relevant to engagement with the Internet and technology. For example, they may wish to consider issues of gender, age, cultural background and familiarity and experience with online communication.

Similar issues may be relevant when considering the best means to recruit participants. It may be a difficult challenge and not necessarily any easier than in a face-to-face setting but by thinking through the challenges of undertaking this research at an early stage can help overcome any difficulties. Researchers must consider the level of technological expertise that potential group participants might have and they must ensure that they have sufficient access to the technology used to conduct the group.

As discussed earlier, researchers need to consider the best type of incentive to encourage participation in the online focus group. Some preparatory work with potential group participants might yield helpful insights into an appropriate reward for participation.

Moderating

Researchers should try to manage expectations from the outset since social norms can vary much more online than in a face-to-face environment. It is vital that participants know what to expect from the group and what is expected from them so as to avoid any unnecessary confusion. This issue is perhaps more salient when conducting synchronous online focus groups. Researchers should make it clear the expectations with regards who should talk and when. In asynchronous groups, guidelines can be issued to participants to tell them how and how frequently they should comment on others' messages (see Box 3.2, Strategies for encouraging participation in asynchronous online focus groups).

With regards the role of moderator, it is vital to be present and visible within the conversations taking place online. Indeed, it is perhaps even more important than in a traditional face-to-face focus group. In the online context, it is important to create a pleasant atmosphere and to ensure that the feel of the group is not impersonal, so first name terms might be appropriate. In asynchronous groups, researchers could perhaps create daily summaries and bullet points to capture the key themes from the discussions and guide further discussion for those participants who do not have a lot of time to read everything.

It may also be advisable, in certain contexts, to have multiple moderators. For example, one moderator could deal with the communication with and between group participants and the other could deal with all things technological.

Online software packages

A number of software packages exist that can offer researchers the opportunity to conduct either asynchronous or synchronous focus groups. Indeed, there are several free packages that might be useful to those on a very limited budget, particularly online discussion forums. As might be expected, those packages that charge offer different levels of functionality and technical support and so researchers should reflect on the specific needs of their project. In particular, packages vary in terms of the number of members that can join an online discussion, the number of administrators as well as the number of discussion boards that can be generated. However, for the purposes of an online focus group some of these issues are arguably less important (Table 3.3).

Table 3.3 Selected chat and forum software packages*

Company	Web address	Pricing
addonChat	http://www.addonchat.co.uk	Free version available, £50 to £260 for professional version, price varies by functionality required
Ning	http://www.ning.com	£18 per month, up to 1000 members, free 14-day trial for all plans
ProBoards	http://www.proboards.com	Free
Realchat	http://www.realchat.com	$295 for 100 users
Second Life	http://www.secondlife.com	Free

* Prices were correct at the time of writing.

Chapter summary

In this chapter, we have considered two broad types of online focus groups, namely asynchronous and synchronous, and have explored some of the potential benefits as well as challenges surrounding their use as a research tool. For researchers, there are many decisions to be made as to which is the most appropriate and many practical and technical issues to consider. Online focus groups can be a useful tool when group interaction and discussion is required but the challenges for both participants and researchers should not be underestimated. The precise nature of the research study, its aims and target population will all need to be considered when designing and running an online focus group. As this chapter illustrates, there are many options available and a number of types of online group platform available to researchers. However, above all else researchers should keep in mind the experience, skills and preferences of individuals in determining which approach to take.

Further reading

Fox, F.E., Morris, M. & Rumsey, N. (2007). Doing synchronous online focus groups with young people: methodological reflections. *Qualitative Health Research*, 17(4), 539–547.

Tates, K., Zwaanswijk, M., Otten, R., van Dulmen, S., Hoogerbrugge, P.M., Kamps, W.A. & Bensing, J.M. (2009). Online focus groups as a tool to collect data in hard-to-include populations: examples from paediatric oncology. *BMC Medical Research Methodology*, 9, 15.

Turney, L. & Pocknee, C. (2005). Virtual focus groups: new frontiers in research. *International Journal of Qualitative Methods*, 4(2), 1–10.

Watson, M., Peacock, S. & Jones, D. (2006). The anlaysis of interaction in online focus groups. *International Journal of Therapy & Rehabilitation*, 13(12), 551–557.

Williams, S., Clausen, M.G., Robertson, A., Peacock, S. & McPherson, K. (2012). Methodological reflections on the use of asynchronous online focus groups in health research. *International Journal of Qualitative Methods*, 11(4), 368–383.

4 Online Surveys

This chapter begins with an overview of the role of surveys in the research process and explains what is meant by an online survey, including reasons why researchers may wish to use this methodology. Next, potential benefits as well as limitations surrounding the use of the online survey are considered. The chapter continues with an overview and discussion of the two most popular forms of online survey, the email survey and the web-based survey and a number of strengths and weaknesses are discussed. Next, the issue of sampling is considered and different types of sampling approaches are discussed together with examples of different types of populations that may become engaged with online surveys. We then turn our attention to sources of error in online surveys and explore the various ways in which error may be introduced into a research study using this methodology. A number of practical and design issues are then discussed and helpful suggestions made as to how best to develop your online survey. The success of any survey rests on ensuring a sufficiently high response rate and we continue the chapter with a discussion of factors that may impact on this. We conclude this chapter with an overview of the role of software packages in the design and running of online survey research.

Surveys

Traditional paper and pencil surveys have long been a part of psychological research and have been used to gather primarily quantitative data about our thoughts, feelings and behaviours. They are especially useful in terms of exploring how widespread a phenomenon is and are a means of gathering large amounts of data, though the degree of depth may be limited (to some extent). Historically, they have used 'tick-box' style responses from participants but often have included open-ended questions. However, the amount of useful data obtained through participants written responses may be limited due to response fatigue. New opportunities have arisen to deliver surveys via the electronic format with the advent of the Internet.

Online surveys

In many ways, the online survey is basically just the electronic equivalent of the paper and pencil traditional survey and many of the same considerations are relevant when thinking about using them. However, researchers now have many more opportunities to engage individuals in psychological research through this new format. Indeed, there are many reasons as to why the online survey may be the preferred format. To illustrate, here are a number of examples though this is by no means an exhaustive list.

1. The Internet may be the subject of study

    The online survey may be used as a means through which to examine Internet use and behaviour. That is to say, this data collection method is chosen deliberately in order to reach a target population with experience of using the Internet. For example, Yau, Potenza & White (2013) conducted an online survey, using online advertisements to recruit participants, in order to examine patterns of Internet use. Specifically, they were interested in comparing individuals whose use of the Internet was deemed problematic compared with those whose use was not. This was achieved by completion of a six item measure which they argued reflected problematic Internet use or 'at risk' online behaviour and how it related to other measures of health and functioning.

2. Characteristics of the population

    There may be particular characteristics of a target population that may make an online survey a useful and relevant tool to collect data. Indeed, there are many online venues where individuals with shared interests and experiences, lifestyles or opinions may come together (e.g. discussion forums, chat rooms and MUDs). Researchers may wish to consider the most appropriate venue through which they can engage individuals in their research study and complete an online survey. One such venue is the online self-help group, which draws together people living with or affected by a specific issue (e.g. depression, unemployment or dental phobia), through which they can share their personal experiences and come together to identify and facilitate strategies to move forward. An example of work using this approach comes from Coulson (2013), in which 249 individuals living within Inflammatory Bowel Disease (IBD) completed an online survey. In this survey, individuals were asked about their illness experience, medical background as well as their use of and views towards IBD online self-help groups. The specific characteristics relevant to this study were that they had to be living with IBD and members of an IBD online self-help group.

3. Exploring personal, sensitive or stigmatized issues

As a result of the anonymity conferred through the Internet, the online survey may be a useful way to gain access to those who have been traditionally hard to reach. Moreover, it may be helpful in eliciting their opinions and experiences and some authors suggest that the online survey is a useful tool when researching sensitive issues or deviant/covert behaviours. For example, in a study by Rosser *et al.*, (2009), an online survey was used to solicit the views of a geographically, racially and ethnically diverse sample of men who use the Internet to seek sex with men. In this case, the anonymity surrounding completion of the survey arguably helped secure a healthy response by 2716 individuals.

4. The attraction of the Internet to particular age groups

It has also been suggested that the Internet may be especially relevant to specific groups, such as young people. Indeed, social networking and Internet use have been shown to be especially common (Internet World Stats, 2013). As a result of this, it may be the case that an online survey may be more positively received since it is being delivered via a platform popular with this age group, that is, the Internet.

Potential benefits of online surveys

There are a number of potential benefits that may arise when using online surveys to research psychological phenomenon.

Some of these have been described in Chapter 1 (e.g. accessing hard to reach groups) therefore only a selected number will be discussed further in the present chapter.

Cost

It may be cheaper to undertake an online survey than doing it by traditional methods such as paper and pencil. Even if the survey is a modest one, the costs of printing, photocopying, mailing and postage can soon mount up and if the survey is on a much larger scale then the costs can be very high indeed. By using an online survey much of these costs are not applicable. However the researcher must still factor in the costs attached to the survey software being used. The price for commercial software aimed at researchers wishing to design, administer and recruit into an online survey varies markedly. These costs may vary depending on the particular design specifications of the survey required, duration and size of the project as well as the services and features required by the software (see Section 'Online software packages'). The good news is that there are several relatively inexpensive (or even free) software tools that can be employed, so even those on a tight budget or no budget at all (e.g. undergraduate psychology project) may be able to employ this online data collection tool. As we shall see later in this Chapter, online surveys can include a range of response formats (see Box 4.1), including open-ended responses, and it is often the case that these (just like any quantitative responses) can be downloaded and made ready for analysis very easily and at minimal cost.

BOX 4.1 Online survey response option formats

There are a number of possible response formats open to researchers who are using online surveys to collect data. The important issue to consider when designing your online survey is that of being consistent throughout with regards font type and size, width of response categories and colour scheme. How the survey respondent interacts with the survey is of great importance and any variation in these design features may lead an individual to attach particular significance to a specific question or section of the survey.

Commonly used response formats

Radio Buttons: A radio button (sometimes known as option button) is an icon representing one of a set of options, only one of which can be chosen at any time. It is typical to use radio buttons as part of a multiple choice. For example

What is your gender?

Male ☐   Female ☐

   Similarly, radio buttons can be presented in the context of a Likert-type scale. They are used when the researcher requires the respondent to choose only ONE option, usually from a selection as illustrated above. Generally, radio buttons are popular and helpful when multiple choice, Likert or other scale questions are being used. Individual software programmes typically offer the researcher the option as to whether response options, such as radio buttons, should be presented horizontally or vertically.

Do you agree or disagree with the following statement about apples?

	Strongly Disagree	Disagree	Neutral	Agree	Strongly Agree
I enjoy eating apples	☐	☐	☐	☐	☐
Apples are good for you	☐	☐	☐	☐	☐
I don't like the taste of apples	☐	☐	☐	☐	☐
I feel full after eating an apple	☐	☐	☐	☐	☐

Check Buttons: These are most likely to be used by a researcher when a survey respondent is allowed to choose more than one option from a list. An example is given below:

In which months do you usually take a holiday abroad?

☐ January   ☐ August
☐ February   ☐ September
☐ March   ☐ October
☐ April   ☐ November
☐ May   ☐ December
☐ June   ☐ None – we don't take a holiday abroad
☐ July

Drop-Down Menus: In this response format the instruction (i.e. question) is visible to the survey respondent but only when they click on the title (or similar) do the actual response options appear. The survey respondent can then move down through the list of options until they identify the most applicable option. Whilst the drop-down menu could be helpful and serve to prevent excessive scrolling, there is the potential for respondent confusion. For example, they may not appreciate fully the length of the drop-down menu.

What is your annual salary? | Select One ⬦ |

(Example of a drop-down menu with an instruction appearing in the box.)

Time

An online survey can save the researcher much time in comparison to the paper and pencil equivalent. For example, at the start of the process the researcher has access to many different software packages that come with readymade survey templates. All that is required is for the researcher to input the particular survey questions as well as response formats required, and 'cut and paste' the necessary participant information, including ethics, and survey instructions. Further time savings can be gained through the actual time it takes to reach potential survey respondents. For example, an online survey can reach a large number of people in a very short space of time, regardless of geographical location. Once the researcher has sent all the recruitment emails/advertising/requests they can then engage with other tasks whilst the data is being collected. Should the researcher be interested, they can also start to immerse themselves in the data as it is being collected. It is very easy to view or download survey responses as they are gathered either through an email, HTML document or other database file. For the researcher, any open-ended qualitative response made by survey participants will not need to be transcribed and therefore this offers an additional time saving to the researcher. The researcher may be able to engage in preliminary data screening or analysis as the survey runs. Indeed, several software packages also have data analysis capabilities and can assist the researcher greatly in understanding their dataset. All in all, the online survey is often found to be a very efficient tool to engage with and can help save valuable time at all points of the data collection process.

Design

As noted previously, there are a number of software packages available that can allow a researcher to easily design and customize their online survey. It is possible to have 'front pages' that convey all the necessary information to potential respondents about the nature of the study as well as what is required from them, their rights as a research participant as well as ethical considerations. Indeed, using software features it is possible to make participants indicate consent through mandatory responses being required for specific questions or statements (e.g. 'Do you confirm that you have read the instructions and are happy to participate in this study?'). In terms of the actual content of the survey, it is up to the researcher how many questions or sections to include in a page as well as whether these pages should be numbered or a progress bar included. It is likely to be appreciated by respondents if at the very least a progress bar is included so that they can monitor their progress with the online survey and hopefully encourage them to complete it fully (see Section 'Designing your online survey').

For those who have used a paper and pencil format previously, it can often be confusing to survey respondents if they have to then move forward several questions or more if they answered 'yes' to a specific question rather than 'no' (e.g. 'If you answered YES to Q8, please go to Page 6, Q11a'). Even if the researcher is convinced everything is clear, there is always the potential for confusion and misunderstanding by respondents. However, with an online survey it is possible to employ an 'if-then' logic with ease and once the respondent has provided their answer to a specific question they are automatically taken to the next relevant question, wherever that may be in the sequence of the survey. Moreover, it is possible to make any or all questions mandatory though it is recommended that the researcher only makes those that are *absolutely necessary* mandatory. The precise set of questions that must be completed will depend on the nature of the study. For example, if a study is exploring gender differences then it makes sense to have the gender question a required question to answer. As noted, the researcher is advised to use these mandatory question functions sparingly since respondents may become frustrated if everything requires an answer. In the spirit of voluntary participation and in line with their ethical rights, it is up to the respondent which questions they feel comfortable answering and whilst the researcher may hope that every question is completed fully, this is ultimately up to the respondent to decide. Some software packages also offer the opportunity to randomize sets of questions or indeed pages/sections of questions. We return to the issue of survey design in Section 'Designing your online survey' and will consider a broader range of design issues.

Potential challenges of online surveys

Whilst the previous section has described some of the advantages to using the online survey methodology, there are a number of potential challenges that must be considered by the researcher. Whilst it is true that some of these issues are also relevant to traditional paper and pencil surveys, there are some issues that are unique to the online setting.

Seen as junk mail

One problem facing the researcher is that the email invitation to participate in an online survey is considered to be spam (i.e. unsolicited junk mail) and therefore potential survey respondents will simply delete it. Moreover, it may be that the mail server itself screens and blocks the email invitation. In 2004, MessageLabs, an internet security firm, revealed that 692 million out of 909 million scanned email messages (76%) sent to its US customers were screened as spam (Evans & Mathur, 2005).

Sample bias

Arguably one of the most frequently debated issues concerning online surveys in psychological research is the issue of sample bias. This bias may arise as a result of the non-representative nature of the Internet population or the self-selection of participants in the study (also known as 'the volunteer effect') or attrition (also known as 'drop out').

In order for an Internet sample to be generalizable to the wider population, the sample must be random and representative. With regards the former, this is a serious issue as it is extremely difficult to obtain a truly random sample. Unlike telephone surveys, that can employ random digit dialling, it is near impossible to create a tool that creates random IP addresses. Indeed, should such a tool be available it would be very difficult to trace this back to a user in such a way as to be able to contact them, not least because of privacy concerns but also because not all IP addresses represent users.

With regards the issue of representativeness, some argue that this issue is becoming less serious as the differences between Internet users and non-users is diminishing. However, there are still some differences that have been reported on a range of socio-demographic and psychological factors (as noted in Chapter 1). We consider issues of sampling later in the chapter (see Section 'Sampling issues').

Privacy and security issues

Those individuals who are invited to respond to an online survey may have a number of privacy and security concerns about doing so. That is to say, respondents may be worried about the security of online transmissions as well as how the data will be used. For example, email surveys (see Section 'Email surveys') do not have a high level of security, attachments can contain viruses and email messages can be intercepted. Furthermore, respondents may be worried about the extent to which their survey responses will be kept confidential or whether personal information may be sold on to other companies.

Multiple submissions

An additional source of bias may result in the same user making multiple submissions. For example, problems can arise if a participant submits their data and then presses the 'back' button in their Web browser to add an extra comment or change one of their responses, thus inadvertently creating a second dataset for the same individual when they press the 'submit' button again (Birnbaum, 2004). Indeed, a number of researchers have discussed this specific issue and suggested that the researcher should check IP addresses (Eysenbach et al., 2004) to determine whether multiple submissions have been made and across what timeline. The rationale for this being that if, for example, the same IP address appears to have submitted 2 survey responses within a 24-hour period, then one of them should be deleted (or both). However, this approach is not altogether helpful because a large number of Internet users have a dynamic IP address (i.e. a different IP address is assigned to the Internet user by their Internet Service Provider each time they log on). Similarly, there are also many Internet users who share the same IP address, perhaps because they are all behind the same router, firewall or proxy. So, whilst checking IP addresses might diminish the problem to an extent, survey respondents may still be able to make multiple submissions. Furthermore, this approach may actually exclude people who have yet to make a survey submission but who may share an IP address with another survey respondent. Other options that have been proposed (e.g. Eysenbach, 2004) include the use of cookies however these can be easily blocked or deleted.

For those researchers that judge this potential problem to be a serious one, the only real way this can be addressed is through the use of unique IDs. A unique ID can be provided to survey respondents in two ways: manual or automatic. In the manual approach, the survey respondent needs to type in the code to login in, whereas in the automatic provision, the URL of the survey link includes the ID. For the former, asking the respondent to type in the ID might increase the number of drop-outs whereas including it in the URL and thereby making its detection automatic, no additional effort is required.

The wrong person may complete the survey

According to Dix & Anderson (2000), it can be difficult at times to ensure that the right person actually completes the online survey. However, the reality is that this potential problem is as much an issue for traditional mail-shot studies and is by no means unique to online research. However, it is fair to say that this problem might be completely eradicated if the study used the unique ID approach described in the previous sub-section.

Collecting data using online surveys

For researchers there are many different options available with regards online surveys and in the next section we shall review two main types: the email survey and the web-based survey.

Email surveys

The email survey is arguably the original form of online survey and certainly the cheapest type. Email surveys are popular because they resemble the traditional paper and pencil type surveys and this may be helpful to respondents because they look familiar. They are very easy to administer and the instructions are often straightforward and accessible. There is a degree of flexibility in the email survey since the respondent is able to change their response if they want to do so (MacElroy, 2000). For researchers, the email survey may be an appropriate tool where there is a very limited budget or where the research study is small scale. Moreover, no particular technical expertise is required beyond that of formatting questions in an email.

Alternatively, the researcher may wish to simply include the survey as an attachment to the email that can be accessed via the respondent's word processing package. However, whilst this approach may allow the researcher the opportunity to undertake more elaborate formatting of the survey there are a number of reasons as to why including it as an attachment may be unwise. First of all, the effort required by survey respondents is greater since they have to open up the attachment, make their responses, save the revised version and email it back to the researcher. Secondly, some respondents may be worried that the attachment contains a virus and may be more reluctant to open the attachment and therefore less likely to engage with the study.

The email survey allows the respondent to reply in whatever way suits them best. For example, they may simply decide to respond on the screen and send their reply straight away to the researcher. For others, they may wish to print the survey and send their replies via postal mail or fax. The researcher should not forget to include this extra information on the survey, just in case.

The speed with which the email survey can operate is impressive. For example, the survey can be delivered to respondents within seconds. Moreover, respondents may decide to just reply there and then once they notice it in their email inbox.

On the downside, the researcher may need to spend quite some time tabulating the email survey results. On the one hand they could simply print all responses and then manually enter the data into a spreadsheet or data analysis package. However, this can be a time consuming task and there is always the risk that some of the data may be incorrectly entered. It is possible, however, to use a professional email survey package that may include analysis services as part of the package. However, using this approach will be dependent on the budget available for the study.

Web-based surveys

The alternative to the email survey is the web-based survey and is arguably more popular with researchers undertaking psychological research. Indeed, a number of benefits arising from the use of web-based surveys are likely to account for this popularity. For example, in a web-based survey the participants are able to 'point and click' and make their responses on various topics with ease. Indeed, the questions and response options offered are likely to be structured and therefore easy for the participant to navigate (see Box 4.1, Online survey response option formats). In addition, the web-based survey allows data transfer and collation via an electronic medium and this may benefit the researcher for a range of reasons, including convenience and data security.

Despite these positive aspects, there are potential limitations and challenges surrounding the use of web-based surveys. However, we shall not be discussing them at this point since these issues are raised in various sections throughout the remainder of the chapter. For now, the main point to note is that there are two main types of online survey, with the web-based survey being the most popular and most frequently used by psychologists.

Sampling issues

Sampling, in the context of online survey research, is an important issue and the researcher has a number of options available to them. The decisions that are made with regards sample selection are crucially linked to the aims and objectives of the research study. For example, in an exploratory study a convenience sample may be sufficient but this may not be the case when there is a need to make statistical inferences about populations. In the following sub-sections, we shall consider two approaches to sampling: probability and non-probability sampling.

Probability sampling

In this approach, the probability of each respondent being included can be calculated. Furthermore, it requires the random selection of respondents from a defined sampling frame and therefore allows the researcher the ability to draw conclusions about population characteristics based on sample statistics. Probability sampling can be divided broadly into two types: closed populations and open populations. Let us look at each of these in turn.

a. Closed populations

   In some situations, the researcher may wish to sample from a detailed and comprehensive sampling frame, such as all members of a charitable organization or employees of an insurance company. In this situation, the researcher needs to determine whether they wish to use a simple random sample, systematic random sample, a stratified sample or a cluster sample (see Box 4.2, Probability sampling procedures for closed populations). In some instances, no sampling frame may be readily available and the researcher must seek to obtain it or create it.

b. Open populations

   In this situation, the researcher does not have any available sampling frame and so to select a probability sample is altogether much more difficult than in a closed population. In this instance, if a random sample of an open population is required, then the researcher would have to use a range of methods to achieve this. For example, they would need to liaise with respondents by telephone (using a random digit dialling approach) and then invite them to log on to the Internet and engage with the online survey.

BOX 4.2   Probability sampling procedures for closed populations

Simple random sampling

A sample in which each and every subset of the population, of a specific sample size, has an equal chance of being selected.

Systematic sampling

A statistical method involving the selection of elements from an ordered sampling frame. The most often use technique is the equal probability method. In this approach, progression through the list is treated cir-cularly with a return to the top once the list is passed. The sampling usually begins by selecting the first item at random and then selecting every *n*th item thereafter.

Stratified sampling

The first step in this approach is to divide the population into homog-enous sub groups (strata). Next, either random sampling or systematic sampling is undertaken in each stratum.

Cluster sampling

This approach is used when pre-existing and 'natural' groupings already are in existence within a statistical population and either random, system-atic or stratified sampling is used to select clusters from the population.

Two common approaches to selecting probability samples from open populations will now be described: pre-recruited panels and intercept sampling.

1. Pre-recruited panels
   A panel of this nature is one that is made up of individuals who have agreed to be available for participation in survey research. This group of individuals is likely to have been recruited through a variety of methods (e.g. face-to-face interviews, email invitations, mail invita-tions, random digit telephone dialling) and are randomly selected to receive an invitation to participate in a specific survey.
   The good news for researchers is that levels of non-response are low, since respondents have all agreed to participate. However, where non-response does occur, it is possible to calculate the rate and compare those who did not respond with those who did, as the researcher will have access to the demographic characteristics of all the panel partici-pants. The degree to which this has been a problem, that can affect the generalizability of the findings, can then be assessed by the researcher.
   In contrast, a problem that researchers may face is that of the 'professional participant' who has become, over time, very skilled at responding to online surveys. The concern here is that they are not very engaged with the actual topic and questions of the study and are simply 'going through the motions'.

2. Intercept sampling

This approach uses pop-up boxes to invite an individual to participate in a specific survey. Such pop-up boxes can be instructed to appear randomly or systematically (e.g. every 10th visitor to a website) and the use of cookies can help prevent multiple invitations to the same individual. As this sampling frame is limited to those who visit a particular website, the researcher must be cautious before generalizing to other populations.

For those researchers considering the use of intercept sampling, a decision must be made as to the optimum time to make the pop-up box visible. For example, if the website visitor is invited to complete the online survey as they arrive at the website then it may be more likely that both those who successfully completed their task online (e.g. finding out specific information) and those who did not will complete the survey. Similarly, non-response may be an issue and the researcher may experience low completion rates, though incentives may help boost rates. Despite these concerns, intercept sampling can be a useful approach in some contexts (e.g. evaluation of a website).

Non-probability sampling

In this approach, random selection procedures are not used and therefore it remains unclear as to the extent to which such samples may or may not represent the population well. As a result, there are many concerns about this approach and some would argue that it should never be used or if they are then only for exploratory research. Researchers should reflect carefully on how serious they view this problem as it may simply be impractical to use probability sampling and it may be beneficial to obtain some data, albeit limited, to explore an issue or topic than none at all.

In those situations where non-probability sampling is being considered, there are a number of approaches available to the researcher. These include: convenience sampling, volunteer opt-in panels and snowball sampling. Each of these will now be described in turn.

a. Convenience sampling

This is a non-systematic approach that allows individuals the opportunity to self-select into the study. Indeed, there are no limits to this and no restrictions as to who can respond. In this case, the online survey is usually posted to a website for all to see and complete. Other convenience sampling techniques might include posting the invitation to complete the online survey to an online community, discussion forum or chat room.

b. Opt-in panels

Opt-in volunteer panels are developed by bringing together a group of participants who have offered to engage with surveys in the future. These individuals are usually recruited through a range of approaches including web-based advertising. As they register they typically provide a range of background demographic data about themselves and then panel members are chosen either through convenience, quota or random sampling to receive the survey. The key distinction between this type of panel and the pre-recruited panel noted in the *Probability Sampling* section is the fact that participants in the opt-in panels have replied to adverts and signed up to engage with surveys. In contrast, the pre-recruited panel is made up of individuals randomly selected from both offline and online populations and invited to join the panel.

c. Snowball sampling

In this scenario, an individual participant is identified and invited to complete the online survey and is asked if they could refer someone else to complete the survey. This process is repeated until the required number of participants is reached. In some situations, this could be a very helpful approach, especially if the research is dealing with populations that have traditionally been hard to reach. This technique is recommended to researchers when the scale of the research is small and respondents are likely to know others that would meet the inclusion criteria for the research study.

Sample size in non-probability sampling

For those researchers who have chosen to use a non-probability sampling approach, the question about sample size is often a common one to consider. In this context, there is no statistical formula that can be used to calculate sample size for the simple reason that it is not possible to know the likelihood of any particular individual being selected for the sample. That is, there is no estimate of the variability in the underlying population and this is an essential piece of information for the calculation of an appropriate sample size.

Sources of error in online surveys

There are a number of potential sources of error that researchers should be aware of when engaging with online surveys. These will now be described in turn.

Coverage error

This type of error occurs when the sampling frame being used does not adequately represent the population of interest. Coverage error is a function of the proportion of the population not covered by the sampling frame that has been developed and the difference between the characteristics of respondents and non-respondents (Couper, 2000).

Sampling error

This type of error occurs when statistical estimates are made based on sample data rather than population data. The actual sample selected for a survey is actually only one of a number of possible samples that could have been selected. The estimates (e.g. means) from each sample can in fact vary from sample to sample as a result of chance. In those instances when the researcher is using a probability sample, variability due to chance in sample estimates can be measured by standard errors of estimates associated with a specific survey.

Non-response error

This type of error reflects the extent to which those selected to participate in a survey choose not to do so. This error is often described in two main ways: unit non-response and item non-response.

a. Unit non-response
   In the case of unit non-response, the respondent does not participate in the survey at all. The unit non-response is determined by dividing the number of individuals who failed to engage with the survey by the total number of potential participants invited to complete the survey. This latter number (i.e. the denominator) must be known.

b. Item non-response
   Item non-response is when the respondent chooses not to complete specific questions in the survey and misses them out. The extent to which this is a problem can be assessed by undertaking item analyses

of all the survey questions. It is possible to undertake descriptive statistical analysis and determine the number of missing cases on each item. Inspection of these cases can alert the researcher to any problem with the survey. For example, if a specific question had an unusually high non-response rate then perhaps the question was considered confusing to participants.

For the researcher, the crucial issue is the extent to which those who choose to participate in the survey differ in a systematic way from those who choose not to complete a survey. If the decision made by individuals were random, then non-response would not be an issue.

Designing your online survey

In contrast to traditional surveys, online surveys have many different possibilities when it comes to the layout and presentation of the survey questions. Furthermore, the decisions that are made with regards design can have a significant impact on how the respondent engages with the survey and so the researcher should always be mindful of this and consider carefully the choices they make. When developing an online survey the researcher should not forget the many valuable lessons that have been learned from traditional paper and pencil surveys.

Dillman (2000) developed a set of useful guidelines that were created to help researchers design online surveys and to hopefully address, to some extent, the sources of error outlined in Section 'Sources of error in online surveys'. These guidelines will now form the basis of the following sections and researchers are encouraged to reflect on each of these suggestions in the context of their own research project and online survey.

1. *Welcome Page:* Introduce the online survey with a welcome page that is motivational and that emphasizes the ease of responding and that clearly explains the actions required for proceeding to the next page. The welcome page is very important and can be used as a means through which to reiterate and reinforce the importance of the study and what it is aiming to achieve, together with an explanation as to why the respondent was invited to participate and to explain any ethical issues, such as confidentiality and right to withdraw. Welcome pages are best when they are

kept relatively brief and are particularly helpful when the online survey is a lengthy one. For those studies that are short, the welcome page and information could be included at the start of the first page.

2. *Access:* Provide a PIN number for limiting access only to people in the sample. The use of a PIN or a password is helpful when dealing with probability samples drawn from closed populations. When the researcher wishes to generalize the results of the online survey to populations, it is vital that only those respondents chosen for the sample actually complete the survey. The danger is that uninvited respondents complete the survey and distort the results. In those instances where a PIN or a password is required, then the researcher may wish to include them in the invitation letter or email. A simple password is encouraged, where appropriate.

3. *First question:* Choose for the first question an item that is likely to be interesting to most respondents, easily answered and fully visible on the first page of the survey. It is important to engage respondents early on in the process since this is likely to be the time in which they may disengage with the online survey. As the respondent moves through the online survey it is argued that they become more invested in it and so the early questions are seen as crucial. In this case, the researcher should pay particular attention to the questions early on and ensure they are not overly complicated or lengthy. Furthermore, the response scales should be easy to use and something that is hopefully familiar to the respondents.

4. *Format:* Present each question in a conventional format similar to that normally used in self-administered paper and pencil surveys. The structure and format of the online survey should be kept as this is seen as being especially helpful to those respondents who are less familiar with the online setting. In so doing, it is likely to encourage completion of the survey both efficiently and accurately.

5. *Colour:* Restrain the use of colour so that figure/ground consistency and readability are maintained, navigational flow is unimpeded, and measurement properties of questions are maintained. Researchers should give some thought to the visual appearance of the survey and reflect upon how respondents may react to different colour schemes. In particular, if the survey is to be offered to an internationally diverse sample then the decision about colour scheme may be even more important. Furthermore, it is vital that the survey has been designed to ensure maximum readability for example dark text on a light background is typically regarded as easy to read.

6. *Visual appearance:* Avoid differences in the visual appearance of questions that result from different screen configurations, operating systems, browsers, partial screen displays and wrap-around text. Researchers should be mindful of technical issues that can impact on the visual appearance of their online survey. It is worth checking the online survey on different browsers as well as different operating systems.

7. *Instructions:* Provide specific instructions on how to take each necessary computer action for responding to the survey and other necessary instructions at the point where they are needed. It is important to write clear, jargon free instructions, regardless of how obvious the required procedure may appear to be. Similarly, for those respondents who may choose not to complete the survey online, then instructions must be provided as to alternative methods to engage with the survey.

8. *Response formats:* Use drop-down boxes sparingly, consider the mode implications, and identify each with a 'click here' instruction (see Box 4.1, Online survey response option formats).

9. *Mandatory responses:* Do not require respondents to provide an answer to each question before being allowed to answer any subsequent ones. In those cases where respondents are asked to complete every question then problems may arise if these questions are personal, not applicable, complex and so on. Furthermore, ethical guidelines suggest that respondents should be free to answer only those questions they wish to. Indeed, in a traditional survey using paper and pencil, the respondent would simply leave blank any questions they did not wish to answer. Similarly for online surveys, the respondent has the right to choose what questions they wish to answer. Naturally, the researcher hopes that a respondent will engage with the online survey as fully as possible but ultimately it is up to the respondent to decide. It is recommended that only a handful of questions are made mandatory, for example, socio-demographic information that can prove useful in describing the sample at a later point in the analysis and write up. If a study does require there to be many mandatory questions then the researcher may wish to include other response options, including 'Don't know', 'Decline to answer' or 'N/A Not applicable'.

10. *Skip directions:* Provide skip directions in a way that encourages marking of answers and being able to click the next applicable question.

11. *Scrolling from question to question:* Construct the online survey so respondents scroll from question to question unless order effects are a major concern.

12. *Response choices:* When the number of response choices exceeds the number that can be displayed in a single column on one screen,

consider double-banking with an appropriate grouping device to link them together.

13. *Progress:* Use graphical symbols or words that convey a sense of where the respondent is in the completion process, but avoid ones that require significant increases in computer memory. For example, a progress bar could be included on each page reflecting the percentage completed thus far (e.g. 25%, 75%). Alternatively, the page number can be included that also states the total number of pages (e.g. page 4 of 10).

14. *Question structures:* Exercise restraint in the use of question structures that have known measurement problems on paper and pencil surveys.

Whilst these guidelines are useful in engaging the researcher in the design process, there may be other design issues that are faced by researchers. Indeed, one common decision faced by researchers who are developing an online survey is whether to have a one page continuous design or spread the survey questions across a number of pages.

In the one page survey design, all the questions of the survey are presented in a single HTML page whereas the multiple page design has more than one page. There are various advantages and disadvantages associated with both designs, according to Manfreda, Batagelj & Vehovar (2002). These are summarized below:

One page design

- Advantages – the respondent is able to view the entire survey; the survey is identical for every respondent; respondents are able to navigate through the survey more easily and this may create a better sense of orientation.
- Disadvantages – the survey is identical for every respondent; respondents may prefer page buttons to move through the survey rather than scrolling.

Multiple page design

- Advantages – server side scripting can interact with the survey respondent each time a page is submitted (e.g. leaving out irrelevant questions, validation of responses, checking for non-responses); order effect can be enhanced since respondents don't see the complete survey.

- Disadvantages – there may be a risk of drop out; response time may be longer; without a progress bar respondents will not know how close they are to the end, grouping questions together may increase correlation; the burden placed on respondents is greater since more action is required.

The difference between these two formats was examined in an online survey of 21,000 undergraduate students. When compared, the authors found that there were few noticeable differences between the scrolling and multiple page designs, including the time taken to complete the online survey. Indeed, after reviewing their findings the authors stated that, 'We continue to hold the view that there is no one best design choice for all survey applications' (Peytchev *et al.*, 2006, p. 604).

Response rates

An important challenge facing researchers who have chosen to use an online survey is that of securing a response rate that is sufficiently high to ensure the quality of the study and to permit appropriate statistical analysis. As the number of studies using the methodology continues to grow, researchers have gained valuable insights into factors affecting responses rates. However, to what extent is response rate a problem for online surveys? A meta-analysis of 45 studies that compared online surveys with other survey modes revealed that, on average, response rates were 11% lower than that of other modes (Manfreda *et al.*, 2008). It would therefore seem that there may be potential problems arising from the use of the online survey in terms of response rate. As a consequence, researchers should consider carefully the possible contributory factors that may have led to this finding and how these relate to their own study. In a systematic review published by Fan & Yan (2010), these factors were considered in relation to four important stages of the survey process. These include: 1) development of the online survey; 2) delivery of the online survey; 3) completion of the online survey and 4) return of the online survey. Let us take a look at each of these in turn.

Development of the online survey

As discussed in the previous section (see Section 'Designing your online survey'), there are many design characteristics that need to be considered when undertaking research using an online survey. However, some of these characteristics have been explored in the context of survey response rates and therefore provide valuable insights for researchers that may be useful in this design process. Three issues have been identified by Fan & Yan (2010) and will now be summarized.

1. Host organization

    A number of studies have reported that the organization that is hosting the online survey can have an impact upon whether potential respondents choose to complete the survey or not. Fan & Yan (2010) conclude that surveys hosted by academic or governmental organizations have higher response rates compared with surveys hosted by commercial organizations. Many software packages allow the researcher to upload an institutional logo that is displayed on the survey.

2. Survey topic

    The topic being researched through the online survey is likely to be an important consideration in the decision by potential respondents as to whether to engage with it or not (Cook *et al.*, 2000; Walston *et al.*, 2006). Indeed, this is the case for mail shot surveys also (Edwards *et al.*, 2002). As might be expected, studies have shown that when the survey topic is of personal relevance (i.e. high salience) then response rates are higher. In addition, if the survey is about a sensitive or non-sensitive topic or whether it focuses on attitudes or facts has been found to relate to response rate (Cook *et al.*, 2000; Edwards *et al.*, 2002).

3. Survey length

    How long a survey is has been found to have a negative linear relationship (i.e. the longer it is the lower the response rate) in both mail shot and online surveys. However, as Fan & Yan (2010) note, the effect sizes reported across studies markedly vary from strong to very weak and a range of explanations have been proposed to account for this. These include: the measures used to report survey length, including the number of questions, number of pages, number of screens as well as the time taken to complete a survey (Cook *et al.*, 2000). Whilst there are many considerations, one suggestion is that a survey that takes 13 minutes or less may be helpful in ensuring good response rates (Fan & Yan, 2010).

Delivery of the online survey

Fan & Yan (2010) present five issues that have been identified in the literature relating to the delivery of the survey to potential respondents and that may impact on response rates.

1. Method of sampling

Online surveys face at least two important challenges in terms of coverage error and sampling error (Couper, 2000). First, not everyone has access to the Internet (i.e. coverage error) and this can result in a biased population. Second, not everyone who has access to the Internet has an equal chance of participating in the survey, due to trips, holidays and access problems (i.e. sampling error). As a consequence, different sampling strategies may yield different response rates. For example, Manfreda *et al.*, (2008) reported that samples consisting of panel members yield higher response rates in online surveys than samples recruited for just a single study.

2. Contact delivery modes

An important early step in the process of conducting an online survey is letting potential respondents know about an upcoming survey or reminding them to complete a survey. There exists a number of potential ways that this can be done such as pre-notifications, email invitations and email reminders. Researchers should consider carefully the best approach to adopt for their survey as these decisions can impact upon response rates. For example, if a potential respondent does not receive an initial email then it is clear to see how this impacts negatively on the response rate. One of the challenges in survey administration is the fact that spam-blocking software may prevent such a survey email getting to the intended recipient. Indeed, it may be the case that the more popular a survey software package becomes, the greater the chance that emails sent from it may be intercepted and blocked by such spam control filters.

Researchers may consider using a variety of methods to advertise and recruit potential participants into their survey. Indeed, creativity may well be the key to success when it comes to response rates and this may involve using different types of adverts, mail shots, telephone calls as well as email invitations. Similarly, researchers may also wish to have available other means through which the survey can be completed, for example, traditional paper and pencil.

Technology may also be used to engage potential participants (e.g. text messaging) and may be a useful means to send reminders to complete a survey. One study conducted by Bosnjak *et al.*, (2008) found that text-message pre-survey notifications (i.e. reminders) resulted in a better response rate compared with email notifications, whereas email invitations fared better than text-message invitations. The highest response rate combined both an email invitation and text-message reminder.

3. Invitation design

In any online survey, the invitation to participate includes a range of information (e.g. survey title, host organization, explanation of survey intent, passwords etc) and some of these have been the focus of research designed to explore response rates. Firstly, the impact of personalizing the invitation to participate has been found to be beneficial. For example, in a study by Heerwegh *et al.*, (2005), using a large student sample, the use of personalized invitations led to a significant increase in response rate of 8.6 percentage points.

An alternative feature that has shown to be helpful is that of scarcity. In a study by Porter & Whitcomb (2003), inclusion of a statement telling the respondent that they had been selected as part of a small group to participate, together with the inclusion of a deadline when the survey website would be shut down, raised response rates by almost 8 percentage points.

The type of access control used in an online survey has also proven to be important. Traditionally, there are three types of control that are used to prevent multiple or uninvited responses (Dillman *et al.*, 1998). These are: manual login in which survey respondents have are asked to type both a username and password to proceed; a semi-automatic login in which a username or a password is assigned; and an automatic login in which a unique identifier is embedded within the survey URL which means respondents do not need to type a username or password to access the survey (Crawford, Couper & Lamias, 2001). Studies have found that the semi-automatic approach to survey access has yielded higher response rates, completion rates, and less socially biased answers to sensitive questions (Crawford *et al.*, 2001; Heerwegh & Loosveldt, 2002, 2003).

In addition, researchers have offered a number of useful suggestions with regards design features that may impact on response rates. These include: identifying the survey task clearly; avoiding attachments and html documents; stating where researchers obtained the email addresses of potential respondents; including a realistic estimation of time needed to complete the survey, including contact information if help is needed and tailoring the invitations to the character of the target populations.

4. Pre-notifications and reminders

A number of experimental studies have demonstrated the positive effects of pre-notification and reminders on response rates, however, the effects have varied across studies (Bosnjak *et al.*, 2008; Trouteaud, 2004). Moreover, the results of several meta-analyses have shown that the number of contacts is one of the key predictors of response rates (Cook *et al.*, 2000; Fox, Schwartz & Hart, 2006). Indeed, it is argued that the pre-notification of the survey to potential respondents is particularly helpful since the decision to access the online survey is largely based on the information provided by the initial contacts (Crawford *et al.*, 2001).

5. Incentives

Incentives have been a common feature of survey research for a long time and have been used as a strategy to increase response rates. Indeed, there has been a considerable amount written about incentives in terms of the different types of incentives, when to offer them and how much (e.g. Goritz, 2006). Whilst traditional paper and pencil surveys may offer a range of incentives, incentives used in online survey research have tended to be electronic. For example, an electronic gift card, redeemable loyalty points, a lottery ticket and so on. One advantage of the electronic gift card may be that only the email address of the recipient is required and hence no address or full name is needed or bank account details.

Completion of the online survey

Various factors are likely to impact upon respondents' completion of the online survey and Fan & Yan (2010) describe these. In the next section we shall consider two such factors: societal and respondent-related factors.

1. Societal

These factors are described as a set of global characteristics in a society that have an impact on survey participation. For example, they include the degree of survey fatigue in society, social cohesion, and public attitudes towards the survey industry. These factors are considered important since they may influence the responses rates to surveys, both online as well as traditional offline surveys. Indeed, in recent years we have witnessed a steady decline in response rates to surveys around the world (Groves *et al.*, 1992). In fact in a meta-analytic study by Sheehan & McMillan (1999), the most important predictor of response rate was the year in which the survey was published.

2. Respondent

Respondent–related factors have been considered in a number of ways. For example, comparing response rates of a single survey across different population groups, how socio-demographic characteristics are related to survey completion as well as personality factors and their role in the decision to complete a survey.

Whilst the evidence is mixed with regards the relationship between these factors and completion of an online survey, two findings are worth mentioning. Firstly, socio-demographic factors are related to participants' Internet resources and computer literacy (e.g. Diment & Garrett-Jones, 2007) so researchers should engage in preparatory work with their target population to determine how these factors may impact on engagement with their online survey. However, there may be little that can be done to address such issues. Even when access to the Internet and computer skills have been controlled for, some studies still suggest socio-demographic factors, such as age and ethnicity, may impact on willingness to complete an online survey (e.g. Couper *et al.*, 2007).

With regards personality characteristics and engagement with online surveys, there is evidence to suggest that those who participate score higher on conscientiousness and agreeableness (Rogelberg *et al.*, 2003).

Survey return

a. Survey return

There exists a vast number (300+) of online survey software products and researchers have many choices to make with regards important features and functionality (see Section 'Online software packages'). Perhaps one of the most important considerations is that the survey software programme chosen supports different browsers (Couper, 2000; Couper *et al.*, 2004; Dillman, 2000). In some instances, the same survey could be displayed very differently to respondents using different computer specifications, browsers,

Internet services and so on. These variations may negatively impact on respondents and they may not be able to browse the survey easily, submit their responses successfully and may even terminate the survey prematurely.

b. Data safety

Participants may be concerned about the security of personal data provided through completion of the online survey. Researchers should be mindful of all aspects of this issue and should guard against hacking, accidental leaking, or careless disclosure of personal data. Researchers may wish to keep identifying information separate to other data, using password protection or encryption, using multiple servers to store parts of the dataset or installing firewalls and virtual private networks (Crawford, 2006a; Kraut *et al.*, 2004).

Online software packages

For researchers, there are many different online survey software packages and online survey services that are available (at a cost). In order to assist the researcher, Table 4.1 lists selected survey software packages available to researchers. This is by no means an exhaustive list and researchers may well find other packages that are available and better suited to their research needs, however, for those unfamiliar with this area then these examples may give you a feel for what is potentially available.

In choosing which software package to work with, researchers may have a number of considerations in mind. Some likely issues to reflect on when choosing a specific software package are those of time, space and number of responses allowed. For example, some software packages may only allow access for a specified period of time (e.g. a month, year) with extra time at an additional cost. Similarly, some companies may charge more for keeping a survey on their server for an extended period of time. In addition, most companies have defined limits with regards number of responses and may charge extra for exceeding this limit (e.g. 1000 responses + additional cost per individual response). Also, there is often varying charges for customer support and researchers should consider very carefully whether they may need support and to what extent (e.g. training).

Table 4.1 Selected online survey software packages*

Company	Web address	Pricing
Bristol Online Survey	http://www.survey.bris.ac.uk	£500 + VAT per year, unlimited surveys and account users
CreateSurvey	http://www.createsurvey.com	$99 per month, unlimited surveys & responses
Cvent	http://www.cvent.com	Price quotes available
FormSite	http://formsite.com	$0–$99.95 per month, depending on number of forms, items and results
Kwiksurveys	http://kwiksurveys.com	Free, unlimited questions and responses. Upgrade at a cost available
PollPro	http://www.pollpro.com	$249 for 1 user, access to server additional fee
Sogosurvey	http://www.sogosurvey.com	Free student licence available, $0 per month, 15 surveys, 75 questions, 200 responses
SuperSurvey	http://www.supersurvey.com	$19.95 single survey, 1000 responses, available for 1 year
Surveymethods	http://www.surveymethods.com	Free to $156 per month, free academic account
Surveygizmo	http://www.surveygizmo.com	$7.99 per month for student, unlimited responses
Surveymonkey	http://www.surveymonkey.com	Basic plan free – 10 questions/100 responses; £24 per month – unlimited questions, 1000 responses/month

* Prices were correct at the time of writing.

Overall, software packages and companies can be of considerable benefit to researchers and have arguably helped the process of developing and conducting online surveys (Wright, 2006). In particular, they can save the researcher a considerable amount of time, especially in terms of designing the online survey. For those researchers with little or no web authoring skills (most of us?) then online survey software packages may be ideal. However, like all studies the researcher must consider their own specific needs and how this fits into their individual circumstances (e.g. time, budget). That said, such software packages may also have some important limitations and researchers should consider carefully whether a specific package may impact on the quality of data obtained. Regardless of which package a researcher ultimately chooses, any challenges with regards sampling response rates, participant deception or access to populations may still remain.

Chapter summary

In this chapter we have considered the main advantages and disadvantages surrounding the use of online surveys and explored the main issue facing researchers who wish to employ this methodology. Despite the many benefits arising from the design options available, researchers need to still consider important issues such as sampling and response rates in order to maximize the potential success of their online survey. However, there are a number of strategies that can be employed to overcome some of these challenges as well as many different software packages that can help in the design and administration process.

Further reading

Dillman, D. A. (2000). *Mail and Internet surveys: the tailored design method.* New York: John Wiley & Sons.

Fan, W. & Yan, Z. (2010). Factors affecting response rates of the web survey: a systematic review. *Computers in Human Behavior*, 26, 132–139.

Goritz, A. S. (2006). Incentives in web studies: methodological issues and a review. *International Journal of Internet Science*, 1, 58–70.

Wright, K. B. (2006). Researching internet-based populations: advantages and disadvantages of online survey research, online questionnaire authoring software packages and web survey services. *Journal of Computer Mediated-Communication*, 10(3).

5 Online Experiments

In this brief chapter we discuss some of the potential advantages and disadvantages of using online experiments. Since there are potentially hundreds of potential experiments that could be designed and conducted online, this chapter will simply summarize some of the key issues that may lead researchers to considering employing experiments for their own research studies. Some useful websites are included for information and readers may wish to explore at their own leisure the vast repository of information contained in such websites.

Experiments

Within psychology, the experimental method has been an extremely influential approach to enquiry and has underpinned much research in our field. At the heart of this approach is the control and manipulation of specific variables as well as trying to establish causal relationships between them.

There have been three main types of experiments conducted within the field of psychology. First, we have the controlled experiment (often conducted in a laboratory or similar environment), which seeks to measure accurately all relevant variables and factors. Second, the field experiment happens in everyday life but the researcher manipulates the independent variable but cannot really control extraneous variables. Third, natural experiments are conducted also in everyday life but the researcher is not able to exert any control of the independent variable.

Online experiments

Online psychological experiments are experiments that are accessed via the World Wide Web and are conducted in the participant's web browser. In recent years, researchers have increasingly begun to conduct a range of different types of online experiment and this trend is reflected in the emergence of websites such as Psychological Research on the Net, Web Experimental Psychology Lab, Online Social Psychology Studies and Online Psychology Research UK that provide links to a growing number of web experiments (see Box 5.1, Online psychological research websites). The use of the World Wide Web as a means for conducting psychology experiments is chiefly due to the increase in availability of Internet access, increase in Internet connection speeds (i.e. broadband) and the development of web-based technologies which allow for a greater degree of interaction between the user and the web browser.

Potential benefits of online experiments

In earlier chapters we have discussed many potential benefits of conducting psychological research online and several of these may also apply to the online experiments. However, in reflecting upon the potential benefits of online experiments for researchers we find that many of them are in some sense a way of overcoming limitations of traditional laboratory-based research. Therefore, in the following section we shall discuss a selection of issues and consider the benefits in relation to potential disadvantages of the traditional setting.

Sample size

Online experiments enable much larger number of participants to be run than laboratory experiments (Birnbaum, 2001; Hewson, 2003; Reips, 2000). This is especially true when the laboratory experiment is conducted at a small institution (Smith & Leigh, 1997). This is because the size of the population pool from which laboratory participants are obtained is considerably smaller than that from which web participants are obtained. Other factors, such as the ability to run participants simultaneously, and at any time, further contribute to larger sample sizes in web experiments. Also, unlike participants for web experiments, participants for laboratory experiments may not always be available (e.g. during the undergraduates' summer recess).

BOX 5.1 Online psychological research websites

Psychological Research on the Net

This site is sponsored by the Hanover College Psychology Department. The website contains many links to active studies across a range of areas including: cognition, consumer, cross-cultural, cyber-psychology, developmental, emotions, environmental, forensic, general, health, industrial, judgement and decision making, linguistics, media, mental health, personality, religion, relationships, sensation and perception, sexuality, social cognition and social issues.

Web Experimental Psychology Lab

This site is maintained by the Psychological Institute at the University of Zurich. The website contains several links to a range of studies in psychology together with some useful information concerning web-based experiments.

Online Social Psychology Studies

This site is maintained by Wesleyan University. This website is full of useful information about social psychology research and teaching. At the time of writing this textbook, it had links to over 285 web-based experiments, surveys and other social psychological studies.

Online Psychology Research UK

This website is maintained by the University of Central Lancashire. It contains links to hundreds of psychological studies online and is an excellent resource for those wishing to learn more about online research methods. It also contains links to several other useful websites that readers may be very interested in browsing.

Sample diversity and generalizability

The demographics of participants in online experiments are more diverse than the demographics of traditional laboratory experiments (e.g. see Krantz *et al.*, 1997). This is because laboratory participants are normally undergraduate psychology students who tend to be predominately female, have the same educational background and are of similar age (Smart, 1966; Schultz, 1972). Furthermore, the prevailing use of undergraduate psychology students may bias experimental findings, especially those of social psychology experiments, since undergraduate students may have less strong attitudes, less formulated sense of self, stronger cognitive skills and stronger tendencies to comply with authority than other adults (see Sears, 1986).

One potential problem that may arise in the use of undergraduate student samples for psychological research is in terms of the generalizability of the study findings. Problems may arise if the results of experiments differ across different populations. In the context of online research, some of the challenges associated with restricted socio-demographic samples (i.e. students) may be overcome. Indeed, it has been argued that psychological experiments conducted online may benefit from a greater diversity in terms of those who choose to engage with the study. As we have learnt previously (see Box 1.1, Access to the Internet and engagement with social networking) and can be seen from recent estimates of Internet penetrance (Internet World Stats, 2013), the socio-demographic profile of Internet users is argued to be approaching that of the general population.

Reips (2000) suggests that since the creation of the Internet and the practice of online experiments, psychologists may be interested in replicating the results of studies conducted under laboratory settings. She argues that such an approach would help to increase the external validity of laboratory-based psychological research.

In addition, online experiments may be a useful means through which to overcome of the main criticisms that has been levelled at laboratory-based research, that is, the inability to generalize findings beyond the study context. Since laboratory-based psychological experiments are likely to be undertaken in highly controlled situations, some critics suggest that the findings cannot be related to the 'real world'. It may be the case that the laboratory is a very artificial or contrived setting and the behaviour and responses of participants does not reflect what would happen in a more comfortable, familiar and naturalistic environment. As a result, advocates of online research suggest that study participants who are undertaking an online experiment are likely to do so in a setting that is familiar, whether this be at work or at home. However, with the increase in access to the Internet on handheld or portable devices, a growing number of psychological experiments can be undertaken while 'on the go'.

A final observation of traditional laboratory-based research is the fact that the majority of this body of work has been conducted during normal working week hours and as a consequence there has been some concern that study findings cannot be generalized outside this timeframe. Indeed, some have suggested that the data generated through traditional laboratory-based research may, in some situations, be influenced by the natural biological rhythms of an individual (Reips, 2000). In contrast, through the Internet participants can undertake online psychological experiments potentially 24 hours per day, 7 days per week, thereby making them more accessible and convenient. Indeed, the issue of convenience is something that has been raised through all of the chapters of this textbook. For those researchers wishing to engage in online experiments, it is extremely easy to log the date and time each participant engaged with the study. In addition, since the online experiment is available outside traditional working hours it is possible to examine whether the findings of traditional laboratory-based research can be generalized outside this timeframe. It should be noted, however, that it is again very easy for researchers to control the display and availability of an online experiment in line with a time-based requirement (e.g. an experiment is only available after 6 p.m. or on weekends only).

Participant bias

As noted in the previous section, much psychological research that has been conducted in laboratory settings has used students as 'volunteers'. There is some concern that in many instances the term 'volunteer' is inaccurate as a student may be offered the opportunity to take part in a psychology experiment and receive course credit or be asked to undertake an essay or other piece of work. In such a scenario, it is not difficult to see that engaging in the experiment might be the preferred option but the student may simply be uninterested in the topic and not motivated to fully engage with the task. In comparison, people who choose to engage in online psychological research may well be more motivated since they have taken the time to read about the study and access the study website.

Experimenter presence and demand characteristics

In online psychological experiments there is no experimenter physically present and therefore data collected in online experiments is free from experimenter bias, (Birnbaum, 2001; Piper, 1998; Reips, 2000). That is to say, the data obtained in online psychological experiments will not be biased by subtle cues to behave in accordance with the experimenter's expectations, which the experimenter inadvertently may give to participants when conducting traditional face-to-face experiments (Rosenthal, 1966). From a financial point of view, the experimenter's absence will make web experiments more cost effective than laboratory experiments, especially if the experiment requires a large sample size, since an experimenter is not paid to conduct each experimental session (see Reips, 2000). Additionally, the absence of an experimenter also increases the participants' perceived anonymity and this may reduce the tendency to give socially desirable answers (Joinson, 1999). Finally, it may also facilitate the collection of personal information of a highly sensitive nature that might not be forthcoming in a traditional face-to-face interaction (Fawcett & Buhle, 1995).

Potential challenges of online experiments

Despite the many advantages that online experiments may bring, there are indeed a number of potential challenges that researchers should consider when embarking upon psychological experiments online. Nearly all of these potential problems have been raised in previous chapters so we will only briefly acknowledge them here.

Levels of control

One immediate challenge facing researchers who wish to undertake online psychological experiments is that of control. Control over each aspect of the experimental process is very important and any problems can undermine the integrity and success of the research project. One common concern is that participants may engage with the online experiment more than once.

Representativeness

As we have noted several times throughout this textbook, there is some concern that the samples that may engage with online research are not representative. This is argued to be the result of differences in access to the Internet but also in the self-selected nature of the sample that chooses to participate.

Attrition

It may be a challenge to researchers to keep participants motivated and engaged in psychological research and so drop-out rates may be a significant challenge.

Chapter summary

For those unfamiliar with online experiments, there are many potential advantages that may make them a viable and helpful option for conducting psychological research. However, they are not without their limitations but none of the challenges described in this chapter are insurmountable problems and indeed as we have seen elsewhere in this textbook there are a number of strategies and actions that researchers can take to address and hopefully overcome these potential limitations.

Further reading

Birnbaum, M.H. (2000). *Psychological experiments on the Internet.* San Diego, CA Academic Press.

Reips, U-D. (2001). The web experimental psychology lab: five years of data collection on the Internet. *Behavior Research Methods, Instruments & Computers,* 33(2), 201–211.

6 Social Media as a Research Environment

This chapter begins with an introduction and overview of the rapidly developing and changing social media landscape. A range of examples of popular online social media activities will be presented along with a discussion of their potential interest and relevance to psychologists, both in terms of research using social media as a data collection tool as well as research about social media as a social phenomenon. Next, the chapter considers the development of social networking and explores some of the potential benefits as well as challenges facing researchers who wish to use it in their research. Following this, we move on to explore the role of discussion forums and how researchers may obtain access to online communities as well as how to generate and analyse data sets using both a text reduction approach as well as in depth analytical approaches. We, then, turn our attention to blogging and its potential as a source of research data, along with the increasingly popular micro-blogging phenomenon (e.g. Twitter). Finally, the chapter closes with a brief overview of the research opportunities relating to YouTube.

Social media

At its most basic level, social media refers to the interaction among individuals in which they create, share and/or exchange ideas or information in online networks and communities. Social media is defined by Kaplan & Haenlein (2010) as 'a group of Internet-based applications that build on the ideological and technological foundations of Web 2.0, and that allow the creation and exchange of user-generated content' (p. 61). In addition, social media rely on web-based and mobile technologies to facilitate and create highly interactive platforms, through which individuals are able to co-create, share, discuss, debate and modify user-generated content. As there are different types of social media, researchers may feel somewhat overwhelmed. However, an extremely useful system was proposed by Kaplan & Haenlein (2010) that classifies social media into six main categories.

Using a set of theories from the field of media research (i.e. social presence, media richness) and social processes (self-presentation, self-disclosure), they were able to systematically classify different types of social media.

According to the social presence theory (Short *et al.*, 1976), media differ in terms of 'social presence'. This is defined as the physical, visual and acoustic contact that can be achieved and the presence that can be reached by two communication partners. Furthermore, social presence is influenced by the intimacy (interpersonal versus mediated) and immediacy (asynchronous versus synchronous) of the medium. Kaplan & Haenlein (2010) argued that social presence can be expected to be lower for mediated (e.g. telephone conversation) than interpersonal communication (e.g. face-to-face conversation) and for asynchronous (e.g. email) than synchronous (e.g. live chat) communication. The higher the social presence, it is argued, the greater the social influence the communication partners have on each other's behaviour.

In terms of media richness theory (Daft & Lengel, 1986), it is proposed that the goal of any communication is to resolve ambiguity and minimize uncertainty. According to the theory, media differ in terms of the degree of richness they possess (i.e. the amount of information that is transmitted in a given period of time). Therefore, some media are better than others at resolving this ambiguity or uncertainty.

With respect to social processes, the concept of self-presentation suggests that individuals are motivated to control the impressions other people may form of them (Goffman, 1959). This is done, in part, to influence others to secure rewards (e.g. positive impression at a job interview) as well as to create an impression that is consistent with one's identity. Similarly, self-presentation is often done through self-disclosure (i.e. the conscious or unconscious revelation of personal information that is congruent with the image one would like to convey).

Using these two sets of processes, the classification proposed by Kaplan & Haenlein (2010) is represented in Table 6.1.

Table 6.1 An illustration of Kaplan & Haenlein's (2010) classification of social media.

		Social presence/media richness		
		Low	**Medium**	**High**
Self-presentation/ Self-disclosure	**High**	Blogs and microblogs (e.g. Twitter)	Social networking sites (e.g. Facebook)	Virtual second worlds (e.g. Second Life)
	Low	Collaborative projects (e.g. Wikipedia)	Content communities (e.g. Youtube)	Virtual game worlds (e.g. World of Warcraft)

In terms of social presence and media richness, blogs and collaborative projects are deemed low as they are typically textual and only permit a relatively simple exchange. Social networking sites and content communities are textual but also allow the sharing or pictures, videos and other materials. Virtual second worlds and virtual game worlds are at the highest with regards social presence and media richness since they endeavour to replicate all aspects of traditional face-to-face interaction but in the virtual world.

With this classification in mind, researchers may be interested to explore the potential of social media for psychological research purposes. Indeed, this could be in terms of using social media as a recruitment tool (e.g. advertising on Facebook to engage with an online survey or posting a link to an online survey in a virtual community discussion forum) or as the topic of psychological research in itself (e.g. exploring the influence of social networking on adolescent risk behaviours).

In the remainder of this chapter, we shall take examples of social media and discuss how they may be used in psychological research. It should be noted, however, that as the social media landscape is vast and constantly evolving, we shall only be selecting a few examples and researchers should bear in mind that the possibilities exist far beyond that which is offered in this chapter.

Blogs

A blog (also known as weblog) is a website that includes a series of regularly updated, reverse chronologically ordered and date stamped posts or entries on a common webpage, typically written by a single author. Blogs usually comprise instant text and graphics publishing, an archiving system arranged and organized by date and a feedback tool through which readers can 'comment' on specific posts contained within the blog. Most blogs are accommodated by software programmes that allow individuals with relatively low technical expertise to design and publish visually engaging and frequently updated online content (Thelwall & Wouters, 2005). Text-based blogs are by far the most common.

'Blogging' has become a popular online activity and this has been driven by the fact that it can be undertaken using free online software (see section 'Online software packages'), coupled with worldwide media reporting of celebrity bloggers (Blood, 2002). The actual number of online blogs remains unclear and different estimates have been proposed. However, a look at some of the more popular online blogging platforms reveals some interesting facts. For example, WordPress.com reports on their 'stats' webpage that there are more than 74 million WordPress sites in existence globally.

Potential benefits of blogs

There are a number of potential benefits that may arise from the use of blogs in psychological research. According to Hookway (2008), blogs can provide a convenient and low cost means through which large amounts of textual data can be accessed. Indeed, it can be considered to be a naturalistic form of data that does not carry the same resource implications compared with face-to-face interviews etc. Second, the archived nature of blogs means that they are available for the analysis of social processes over time as well as providing insights into everyday life.

In his own work in exploring how contemporary urban Australians experience morality in their everyday lives, Hookway (2008) reflected on how best to undertake this study and to empirically examine this issue. One potentially obvious means of data collection was that of the diary and while it can often be of value in collecting sensitive information as well as information over time, there are challenges in terms of engaging partici-pants in such an activity. After reflection, Hookway (2008) decided to use a blog approach and argued that 'Weblogs offer a viable alternative, giving diary researchers the best of both worlds. On the one hand, blogs help overcome issues of finding and accessing unsolicited personal diaries, while on the other hand, they are not "contaminated" by the predating interest of a researcher.' (p. 96).

Researching in the blogosphere: some issues to consider

Using blogs in psychological research may be unfamiliar to many readers. In this section, we learn from the experiences of Hookway (2008) and provide some helpful basic steps for researching in the 'blogosphere' (p. 98).

Searching for relevant blogs

The first step facing the researcher is to search for, identify and select relevant blogs to be used in the research project. A vast majority of blogs are hosted by content management systems and researchers should consider reviewing these as an initial and preparatory stage in the process. For those less experienced with blogs, a simple online search will similarly yield many relevant examples of blogs and content management systems. It is worth spending some time simply browsing through and considering the various examples and types of blogs available online. Indeed, some content management systems have a search function that will allow readers, in this case researchers, the opportunity to search for blogs according to some specific criteria (e.g. country). Researchers should consider whether they require blogs of a specific type and explore different con-tent management systems to ascertain whether the appropriate search can be undertaken (Box 6.1).

BOX 6.1   Why do people blog?

Summary of research from Nardi, B.A., Schiano, D.J., Gumbrecht, M. & Swartz, L. (2004). Why we Blog. *Communications of the ACM*, 47(12), 41–46.

Background

The majority of blogs are written not by journalists or politicians, but by ordinary people, and this study sought to explore some of the motivations for blogging. A series of interviews were conducted with 23 adults (16 men and 7 women), aged from 19 to 60, belonging to New York or California, USA. They belonged to middle class, were well educated and were either in education or working and enjoyed blogging. These interviews were semi-structured and were undertaken in conjunction with a review of the relevant bogs as well as email and instant messaging follow-up discussions.

Findings

Through their analysis of the interview transcripts, coupled with a review of the content of blogs, five key motivations were identified for blogging. These will now be briefly summarized:

1. Blogs to 'document my life'
   Several of the interviewees reported blogging to record activities and events, sometimes being done to inform and update others about their activities and whereabouts and often included photos. The blog could be a public journal, a photo album or a travelogue, depending on the audience and content.
2. Blogs as commentary
   Blogging also appeared to give a voice and allowed people to express their opinions and viewpoints, particularly with regards issues they found pertinent and important. The interviewees reported blogging about a range of topics, for example, an academic conference and the impact of DVDs.
3. Blogs as catharsis
   Several in the sample described how they blogged as an outlet for thoughts and feelings, sometimes generating emotional content. Blogs were written, sometimes, to work through feelings or to express frustration.

> In other instances, they were used to explore issues the author felt passionate about.
> 4. Blogs as muse
>   Some described the way blogging allowed them to think and test out ideas through writing.
> 5. Blogs as a community forum
>   Many individuals expressed their views to one another in community settings. Indeed, several different types of community were described including work groups, poetry groups and student groups.

Sampling blogs

Researchers wishing to sample blogs according to some specific criteria (e.g. location, age, hobby or interest) can use the search function as outlined previously. However, it should be noted that different content management systems may differ in the search criteria that can be used. Despite this, researchers may be able to exploit this search function in order to undertake purposive sampling. For example, a researcher may be interested in identifying blogs discussing the experience of quitting smoking or perhaps blogs describing the experience of workplace bullying. There are some websites that are useful in terms of searching for blogs that may be hosted across various content management systems. For example, Technorati is an Internet search engine for searching blogs and does this through searching the tags that bloggers have used to describe the content of their blogs. It indexes more than one million blogs and not only does it track the authority and influence of blogs, it also provides the most comprehensive and current index of who and what is the most popular in the Blogosphere.

Preparing the data for analysis

Since the vast majority of blogs are textual, researchers may find that it is relatively straightforward to prepare the data for analysis. Indeed, this may be as simple as copying and pasting text into a qualitative analysis software programme (e.g. NVivo). However, it is likely that some basic editing or tidying up of text will be required before submitting it to computerized data analysis techniques.

Microblogs: the example of Twitter

Microblogging has become an incredibly popular tool among Internet users and is an important source of information with approximately 340 million new tweets (i.e. the name given to the texts posted to the site that are <140 characters in length) and 1.6 billion search queries occurring every day (Rui et al., 2013). Consequently, microblogging sites such as Twitter have opened up new opportunities for psychologists and there are several reasons as to why such platforms may be useful for research. First, microblogging sites are used by many people to express their viewpoints and personal opinions about a diverse set of topics. As a result, it provides a unique opportunity for psychologists to explore public opinion including analysis of such opinions over time (i.e. longitudinal analysis). Second, there is a huge amount of tweets that can be included into a dataset and therefore available for analysis. Third, a broad range of people choose to use Twitter (e.g. ordinary members of the public, politicians, celebrities, athletes and so on) and so it is possible to examine tweets from different social groups with different interests. Indeed, the use of Twitter is worldwide though the vast majority of users are located in North America, Europe, Australia and South America (Kriek *et al.*, 2011).

For those wishing to study the content of microblogs such as Twitter, there are, in fact, a range of tools that can be used. These tools vary in the amount of technical expertise required to use them but there does exist some free, easy-to-use data mining software tools online (see section 'Online software packages' and Box 6.2).

BOX 6.2   Example of analysis of Twitter

Summary of research from Chew, C. & Eysenbach, G. (2010). Pandemics in the age of Twitter: Content analysis of Tweets during the 2009 H1N1 outbreak. *PloS One*, 5(11), e14118.

Background

In June 2009, the World Health Organisation (WHO) declared the new strain of swine origin H1N1 (also called 'swine flu') a pandemic. In order to examine public opinion and behavioural responses to such public health emergencies, previous methods (e.g. telephone interviews, Internet and face-to-face surveys) were considered to be seriously limited as a result of the timeline involved. For example, even a paper and pencil survey needs planning time, funding, piloting and then distribution and collection of data. It was against this backdrop that the authors undertook a novel study that harnessed online textual data via Twitter. It was felt that mining Twitter data would provide an instantaneous insight into how the public were responding to the unfolding pandemic. In particular, it was seen as useful in providing a longitudinal analysis of changes in opinions or behavioural responses and the data obtained could provide both a quantitative examination as well as a qualitative one.

Methods

An open-source system was developed that collected and mined textual information from Twitter via its Application Programming Interface. Every few seconds, Infovigil mined for new public domain tweets using keywords specified by the authors. From 1 May to 31 December 2009, the system mined over 2 million tweets using keywords or hasthtags (#) 'H1N1', 'swine flu', and 'swineflu'. In addition they recorded the cited webpages.

Findings

The results revealed that tweets using 'H1N1' increased from 8.8% to 40.5%, suggesting that the public were taking on board the terminology recommended by the WHO. In addition, the results found that resource-related posts were the most commonly shared (52.6%) and that twitter activity peaked during high profile media news stories.

Social networking sites

Since their introduction, social networking sites (e.g. Facebook, MySpace, Bebo) have attracted many millions of users who have integrated them into their daily lives and routines. Many social networking sites exist, each with a similar (more or less) set of technological features but often with quite varied cultures and group dynamics. Many social networking sites (e.g. Facebook) bring together individuals in already existing social networks but other sites draw complete strangers together through a shared interest in a particular lifestyle, interest or political opinion. As a consequence, sites will vary with regards member composition with some drawing together diverse groups of people whilst others will have a fairly homogenous group composition, perhaps based on a specific national identity or racial, sexual or religious identity (Boyd & Ellison, 2008). Sites may also vary according to the types of communication and information features they include such as mobile connectivity, blogging or photo/video sharing.

In essence, social networking sites can be described as online systems and services that permit individuals to create their own profile that may be public or restricted in some way. Furthermore, they allow the articulation of a list of other individuals with whom a connection is shared and this list can be viewed and accessed. It should be noted, however, that the way these connections are labelled or described across different social networking sites may vary from site to site.

One of the key features of social network sites is the fact they permit individuals to express and make their social networks visible. Consequently, connections can be made between individuals who would probably not otherwise have met each other, but this is seldom the aim, and such connections are usually between 'latent ties' (Haythornthwhaite, 2005) who share some form of offline connection. Social network sites provide the opportunity to make visible profiles that display a list of 'friends', all of whom are also users of the particular site. Each profile is a unique page where individuals can describe themselves according to a range of socio-demographic characteristics and other relevant attributes. Many sites also encourage users to upload a picture of themselves or other multi-media content.

Arguably, one of the key ways in which social network sites differentiate between each other is around issues of visibility and access. For example, profiles on sites such as Tribe.net are crawled by search engines and so are visible to anyone regardless of whether an individual has an account or not. In contrast, LinkedIn restricts what a person can see depending on whether they have a paid account. Sites such as MySpace allow users the opportunity to decide whether they wish their profiles to be public or restricted to just 'friends only'. In contrast, Facebook makes profiles visible, by default, to friends of users, that is, their network, unless a specific user has denied an individual the ability to view their profile.

Once an individual has joined a social network site, they are often asked to identify others with whom they share a connection. These connections may differ in terms of how they are described for example they may be called 'friends' or 'contacts'. Typically, a user will have to confirm the existence of this connection before the structural relationship on the site is confirmed. It should be noted that the term 'friends' may be misleading, as it is not in the sense that we might think (Boyd, 2006) and indeed there may be many diverse reasons individuals connect within a social network site.

A fundamental aspect of social network sites, according to Boyd & Ellison (2008) is the fact that there is a public display of connections. Through the links to each friend, a user can see the profile of each person in the list of connections. An additional feature, seen in most sites, is the ability to leave a message or write on their friends' profiles. In some sites, there is also a private mail function but this feature is by no means a common one (Box 6.3).

BOX 6.3   Social network sites: a brief history

According to Boyd & Ellison (2008), the first social networking site was launched in 1997. This site was called SixDegrees.com and provided users with the opportunity to create a profile, list their friends and from 1998 browse that list. Whilst Boyd & Ellison (2008) note that each of these functions were in fact available prior to this date, via instant messaging programmes such as AIM or ICQ, it was the first to combine them all together. SixDegrees.com was designed to help people connect with and send messages to each other. However, it failed to become a sustainable business despite attracting many million users and closed in 2000.

In 2002, things really gathered pace when Friendster was launched. This site used the concept of degree of separation, similar to that of the closed SixDegrees.com, and refined it into a routine called the 'Circle of Friends' (where the pathways connecting two people are made visible), and put forward the idea that a rich online community can only exist between people who truly have a common bond. This site grew quickly, with over 3 million users just one year after it was launched.

A different, and perhaps more serious approach was taken, by LinkedIn which launched in 2003. Rather than being a space for chitchat and friends to link with each other, this site was launched as a networking resource for business people who wanted to connect with other professionals. It is estimated that LinkedIn has in excess of 180 million users and continues to grow in popularity.

Launched in 2003, MySpace is altogether much more popular as judged by almost three times as many users as LinkedIn. This site, while not the most popular one globally, remains popular among the youth in North America and is often used to share music, videos and generate other media rich content.

In 2004, Facebook was launched with the original aim of connecting US college students. It began with Mark Zuckerberg's alma mater Harvard and membership could only be gained by being invited by a member of Facebook. Such an 'exclusive' network proved to be highly successful and within a month, approximately 19,500 students at Harvard signed up. After about two years Facebook went public and in 2008 it surpassed Friendster and MySpace as the leading global social networking site. Recent estimates suggest Facebook has in excess of 975 million members worldwide (Internet World Stats, 2013).

Potential benefits of using social networking sites in research

As a result of the increasing popularity of social networking sites, there are a number of potential benefits to researchers. While some of these potential benefits are similar to those described earlier in this book, there is some value in reiterating these since some researchers may not be familiar with the potential of social networking sites to undertake psychological research.

Accessing hard to reach populations

Social networking sites may help a researcher access a segment of the population that has been traditionally difficult to reach. It may be the case that undertaking random sampling is near impossible and therefore a snowball sampling design is used whether one participant refers the researcher on to another. In the context of social media, members of social networking sites may well know each other and be able to refer the researcher quickly on to several others.

A source of naturalistic data

Social networking sites may represent a plentiful and rich source of naturalistic behavioural data that lends itself to 'cyber-ethnographic' research. Indeed, some researchers draw similarities with research that uses diary entries as a tool to collect data (Leng, 2013). It is argued that social networking sites provide a regular flow of 'undirected' data which may also be used for temporal analysis. For example, researchers may be interested in how users construct meaning over time and how attitudes may evolve through online interaction with other users (Golder *et al.*, 2007). Furthermore, it is suggested that since messages posted by users of social networking sites are highly reflective of their experiences, they are less likely to be distorted and therefore more valid (Broderick, 2008).

Potential challenges of using social networking sites in research

There are many potential challenges arising from the use of social networking sites and we now consider a selection of these.

Generalizing to the general population

A key issue when considering the use of social networking sites in psychological research is whether the results can be generalized to the wider population. It would appear that the central concern is whether there exists any differences between those who engage with social networking sites and those who do not. A number of studies have been undertaken that explores the use of social networking sites and some evidence suggests there is indeed some demographic differences (Peluchette & Karl, 2008). It would appear that users of social networking sites tend to be younger than non-users and, therefore, this calls into question the extent to which they represent the wider population. In addition, there are also differences between users and non-users of social networking sites with respect to Internet access as well as being more familiar and comfortable with the technology (Anderson *et al.*, 2012; Hargittai, 2008). However, the number of people accessing the Internet continues to grow (Internet World Stats, 2013) and so it could be argued that these differences will dissipate over time. That said, where Internet access is restricted to specific geographical locations or those with higher incomes, there will be a problem with regards the generalizability of research findings based on research social networking sites.

Another area where researchers have been exploring whether any differences may exist is with regards personality characteristics and other psychosocial characteristics. While Gangadharbatla (2008) reported that members of social networking sites have a greater need to belong to a social group, this finding has not been replicated across other studies. In a recent review by Anderson *et al.*, (2012), it was concluded that there was insufficient research evidence to suggest that there are personality differences between users and non-users of social networking sites.

Activity level

Researchers should be cautious while considering the use of social network sites for their research that there exists a sufficiently high level of online activity to make analysis meaningful. In some instances, a social network site may not contain many users and there may be little interaction between users thereby calling into question the representativeness of any views that may be expressed. However, it is not only the volume of messages that are posted to a social networking site but also the quality of those messages that researchers should consider. For example, messages may be short when posted to social network sites and this may be a challenge to researchers in terms of undertaking any meaningful analysis. Similarly, users who post messages may not have sufficiently capture a particular viewpoint, experience or attitude in sufficient depth to successfully analyse. However, where researchers may benefit is with regards the analysis of messages posted to a social networking site over time. Leng (2013) argues that the 'temporal analysis allows researchers to form a theory as to how attitudes or behaviour may change with time or in response to other members in the social network' (p. 687).

Validity of messages posted

In many instances, the content of any message is likely to be accurate and truthful since users interacting with each other are likely to know and trust one another. As a consequence, their messages provide a source of valid data concerning an array of thoughts, feelings, opinions and experiences. However, researchers should be aware that there does exist the potential for messages to be unreliable and dishonest especially when discussing socially undesirable behaviours, as there may be pressure to conform to group expectations and norms. Moreover, users may be less willing to be truthful about a behaviour or opinion that may embarrass them so researchers should be mindful of this when considering the use of messages as part of their dataset.

Group online social networking (i.e. virtual communities)

A group (also known as a community or e-group) is a feature in many social networking sites that allows users to create and post, comment on and read from their own interest specific forums. Such groups may be closed (i.e. a user must register a valid email to be able to read and actively contribute through posting messages) or open (i.e. the content of the forum is publicly available). In the same way as mailing lists, forums are looked after by administrators, moderators or owners who have the administrative rights to be able to edit or remove messages posted to the group as well as regulating member behaviour.

Online forums (also known as bulletin boards or message boards) have rapidly increased in both prevalence and popularity as social networking technology advances. Indeed, there are forums on almost every conceivable topic representing all aspects of living (e.g. TV programmes, dieting, cultural groups, workplace, travel and so on). As a result of this growing online presence, an increasing number of researchers in the field of psychology have analysed data derived from these forums, myself included.

In Chapter 3, we first introduced the concept of the online forum and briefly described their structure. To remind ourselves, an online forum is quite simply just an online discussion site. They typically have a tree like structure that can sometimes be organized into specific sub-forums or thematic sections. For example, a breast cancer online forum may have different sections or sub-boards dedicated to a range of issues including treatment, employment, caregivers etc. In reality, there is potentially no limit to the number of sections or sub-boards contained within an online discussion forum; however, the researcher should be mindful that the precise structure is likely to vary from site to site and they should always take the time to familiarize themselves with the site and its layout and structure.

Potential benefits of using online forums

There are a number of potential benefits to the researcher from engaging with online forums in order to undertake psychological research. These benefits can be described as follows:

Vast amount of online material

It is hard to quantify the number of online forums in existence since hundreds of new ones are likely to be created every day. Similarly, it is near impossible to provide an accurate estimate of the number of people contributing to such forums and the amount of online discourse that exists and potentially available to researchers. However, for those perhaps unfamiliar with them and unable to comprehend their size, an online forum can potentially have several thousands of registered members and as a result there may be thousands of conversation threads and several million posted messages. It is worth noting that the actual size and composition of each forum is likely to vary depending on its focus, aims and purpose. For the researcher, identifying a potential forum is unlikely to be a difficult task and even those that are modest in their size may still yield sufficient data to undertake a meaningful analysis. The challenge may rest in deciding which from potentially hundreds of forums to choose from but these issues will be considered later (see Section 'Working with online forums: a step-by-step guide').

Naturally occurring online conversations

Discussions that take place within online forums can be of great interest to the researcher since they can be seen as naturalistic. That is, members of the community engage in discussion about the specific topic (e.g. political views, hobbies, chronic illness) without any researcher being present and potentially influencing the online interaction. Moreover, the anonymity conferred through the Internet often helps individuals to speak more freely within online forums. Indeed, it can be argued that they may be less influenced by social desirability than might have been the case in focus group or interview settings.

Opportunities for longitudinal studies

Since online forums comprise messages posted by members over extended periods of time, researchers have a unique opportunity to conduct longitudinal studies. For example, in the health field, one may be interested in exploring the accounts of selected group members recently diagnosed with a particular condition (e.g. breast cancer) and exploring how this impacts upon their identity as judged by the messages posted to the forum.

Potential challenges of using online forums

Anonymity

While anonymity may have a number of potential benefits to the research, it is often a double-edged sword. For example, little is often known about the individuals who are participating in the forum discussion. Typically, any socio-demographic information is very limited and may vary from forum to forum. For example, one forum might have member profiles together with usernames (e.g. mickeymouse123, male, 43 years old, United Kingdom) whereas other forums may simply show the username. Where socio-demographic information is presented, there is no way to verify it and this presents challenges to the researcher in terms of describing the origins of the data being used for research purposes. That said, it is usually possible to offer a description of the forum with regards its overall aims and functions. The extent to which anonymity may present a problem to the researcher will ultimately depend on the specific aims of the research study.

Representativeness

Representativeness is a key problem facing researchers working with data derived from online discuss forums. The problem is that they are not able to make any solid claims with regards the representativeness of a particular population. Those who participate in discussion within the online forum may not be representative of those who have access to the Internet. Similarly, those who have access to the Internet may not be representative of the particular population of interest.

Working with online forums: a step-by-step guide

1. *Identifying and selecting relevant online forums*

The first step facing the researcher is to search for, identify and select relevant online forums to be used in the research project. The precise nature of the research question will influence much of the preparatory decisions made. For example, a researcher may be interested the experience of men within the United Kingdom who are living with prostate cancer. In this instance, the search terms used should include some reference to the UK. However, it is likely that far more possible forums will be identified, regardless of the search terms; the researcher should then screen these forums for relevance to the study. It should be pointed out that when working with online forums, and using the example of prostate cancer, the search results might yield a general cancer online forum but there may be a section or sub-board that is dedicated to men in the UK living with prostate cancer. Similarly, different search engines might potentially yield slightly different results and the researcher may wish to consider using multiple engines to undertake this initial search. In the case of a project looking at prostate cancer in the UK, the researcher must also be mindful of the fact that a range of different terms might be used to represent the forum. For example, search terms could include the following: prostate cancer + online support group or online support community or bulletin board or message board or virtual forum.

Next, the researcher may wish to consider which of the possible online forums they should use within their study. One suggested approach might be to examine each of the forums identified (if this number is not too great) and record the size of the forum, its structure (i.e. sub-boards), the number of messages and level of activity. This can help the researcher discount any forums that perhaps are too small (e.g. less than 50 members) and that might generate too little data (e.g. less than 1 message a day). In some ways, it is better to opt for those with larger numbers and a higher volume of message activity than struggle to have enough data. However, the particular research question will ultimately dictate many of the decisions made at this early point.

2. *Selecting relevant forums, sections and sub-boards*

With a list of potential forums (or sections/sub-boards) that satisfy the requirements of the research study, the researcher must decide how many of these to include. If, for example, they are all very large indeed with a vast number of conversation threads and thousands of messages then a decision may need to be made based on practical limitations. It may simply not be possible to include all the forums in the study and so if the project is time restricted to a few months (e.g. an undergraduate or M.Sc project), then the researcher may wish to consider using just 1 or 2 forums. If the researcher has a longer time frame through which to engage with the project then it may be worth considering using multiple forums to address, at least somewhat, earlier concerns about representativeness.

In terms of which sub-boards to include in the project, the research question again will be crucial in this decision. To illustrate, in a study by Malik & Coulson (2010a) that aimed to explore the provision of self-help mechanisms within a UK based infertility online support community, 500 messages from 7 sub-boards were selected for analysis. The decision to sample messages from 7 sub-boards was taken in order to reflect the fact that infertility is a journey and there may be different issues salient at different points of that journey. For example, in their study they selected the following sub-boards: 'starting out', '2-week wait', 'negative cycle', 'in between treatment', 'trying for another miracle', 'pregnancy loss' and 'moving on'. Similarly, the researcher who is wishing to examine the impact of prostate cancer on sexual functioning may identify relevant sub-boards (should they exist) that deal with that specific issue.

3. *Deciding on which conversation threads to use*

A number of factors may impact on the decision as to which conversation threads to download for analysis, though the research question is clearly going to be the main consideration. For example, a researcher may be interested in all threads generated within a specific time period (e.g. January to June) and will download those threads for potential analysis. Alternatively, they may not have any specific time frame in mind but rather wish to sample from the many conversations present online. In such a scenario it is advisable to undertake random sampling of the conversation threads such that each thread has an equal chance of being included in the data set. Such a strategy will help to ensure that both shorter and longer threads (e.g. 3 replies, 147 replies), generated at different time points, with varying numbers of contributors are included. To do this, the researcher may wish to number each of the conversation threads (e.g. 1,2,3,4....) and then using a random number generator select conversation threads to be included (provided they meet the inclusion criteria for the study). The dataset will then include all messages within the threads selected for analysis. The number of messages so yielded is likely to vary from one forum to another; however, such a strategy is recommended.

The researcher must then consider how many conversation threads to use for analysis. Naturally, the number of messages within each thread is important and there is no recommended number of threads and/or messages in this type of research. Rather, the researcher must use some other criteria upon which to make this judgement call and here saturation may be the solution. Simply put, saturation is the point where no new important insights are gained from the analysis.

4. *Preparing the data for analysis*

It is unlikely that the data generated through the process outlined so far will result in a dataset that is immediately ready for analysis. Indeed, there may be a number of preparatory actions that must be taken to ensure the dataset is fit for transfer into a software package (or by hand for the very brave). The researcher is advised to download the text into an appropriate word processing package and backed up immediately. Next, any redundant features of the website copied into the package should be deleted leaving just the core material that will be the focus of the analysis. Again, the specific features retained will be determined by the specific research question for the study and whether their inclusion may help the researcher gain an insight into the particular topic being investigated.

Many forums also allow previous messages in a conversation to be included in later replies. For the researcher, this means there is potentially much duplication in content and an inflated word count. Again, the seriousness of this issue is likely to be determined by the interests of the researcher. For example, if the researcher is interested in interaction patterns between members of an online forum then this is not really a problem. If the researcher deems that it is a problem then they need to remove this content either via the word processing package or by hand.

As the forum is likely to yield a table format when the conversations (and messages) are downloaded, this needs to be addressed also and the material converted to plain text.

Analysing data from online forums

The researcher has many options available when it comes to the analysis of online discussion forum data. So far in the psychological literature, there have been two broad types of data analysis undertaken – text-reduction and in-depth analysis. Let us have a look at these with some examples in order to illustrate the potential that exists within such online spaces.

Text-reduction approaches to data analysis

In this approach, the aim is to 'reduce' the data into a set of meaningful themes or concepts, through for example, content analysis. For those researchers interested in undertaking content analysis on their dataset then one important decision that needs to be made is that of unit of analysis. Holtz *et al.*, (2012) suggests that the single posting (i.e. message) should be considered as the unit of analysis in online discussion forums. They argue that the posting is a natural transition in a communicative exchange within forums. As a consequence, the researcher will examine each posting for evidence that it contains elements that represent the category or concepts of interest (Box 6.4).

BOX 6.4 Example of text-reduction analysis of online forums

Summary of research from Coulson, N.S., Buchanan, H. & Aubeeluck, A. (2007). Social support in cyberspace: A content analysis of communication within a Huntington's disease online support group. *Patient Education & Counseling*, 68, 173–178.

Background

Huntington's disease is an inherited degenerative disorder affecting the brain that currently has no cure. As a consequence, patients and those in their social network (e.g. family and friends) often experience high levels of anxiety and psychological distress. Since the advent of the Internet, those affected by Huntington's disease have new opportunities for seeking information, advice and social support. The aim of this study was to explore the provision of social support within messages posted to a single Huntington's disease online discussion forum that supported individuals affected by the condition.

Development of the coding frame

The study employed the social support behaviour code that was originally developed by Cutrona & Suhr (1992) and was adapted to meet the needs of the online nature of the study (e.g. an item in the framework 'listening' was removed from the coding framework due to the fact it was not possible for group members to physically listen. Similarly, 'physical affection' was altered to 'virtual affection' to recognize the fact that members could not physically interact but that including virtual acts of affection such as <<<<<hugs>>>>> was commonplace). The framework included five main types of social support: emotional (i.e. communicating love, concern or empathy), informational (i.e. providing information or advice), esteem (i.e. communicating respect and confidence in abilities), network (i.e. communicating belonging to a group to a group of persons with similar experiences or concerns) and tangible assistance (i.e. providing or offering to provide goods or services) with 22 subcategories within these.

After the data was coded (i.e. $n = 1313$ messages), the authors reflected on the coding framework and decided that there was much overlap between the subcategories 'validation' and 'empathy' and were therefore combined and recorded as validation/empathy under the emotional support main category. In addition, it was felt that there existed a new subcategory that reflected the group's unique position to share experiences and this was coded as 'anchorage' under the esteem support main category. The subcategory, 'relief of blame', was viewed as representing emotional support as opposed to esteem support and the subcategory, 'express willingness', was coded as network support as they represented a general willingness to help other members of the group rather than a specific tangible act. Each message was rated by two individuals and reliability was computed based on the five main categories (Cohen's Kappa ranged from .86 to .94).

Results

The results of the content analysis revealed that social support was present in 98.9% of the messages ($n = 1299$) and the table below describes the specific findings with respect to each main category and the 22 sub categories.

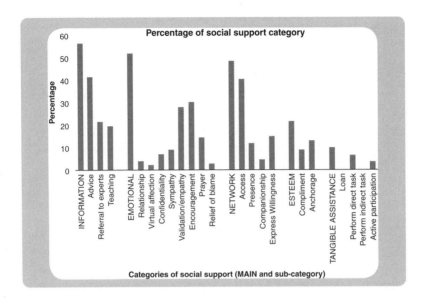

In depth approaches to data analysis

In contrast to the previous reductionist approach, it is also pos-sible to undertake a range of qualitative analysis techniques to forum data, such as thematic analysis (Braun & Clarke, 2006) or Interpretative Phenomenological Analysis (Smith *et al.*, 2009). Researchers may have a variety of interests that make in depth qualitative analysis appropriate though it should be noted at this point that there is likely to be an abundance of rich data available and so decisions will need to be made about just how much data to include in any in-depth analysis being undertaken (Box 6.5).

BOX 6.5   Example of in-depth analysis of online forum

Summary of research from Malik, S.H. & Coulson, N.S. (2008b). The male experience of infertility: A thematic analysis of an online infertility sup-port group bulletin board. *Journal of Reproductive and Infant Psychology*, 26(1), 18–30.

Background

Past research has illustrated the fact that men and women differ in their response to the experience of infertility. However, there is comparatively little research that has focussed on the male experience of infertility. Therefore, the aim of this study was to examine the communication within an infertility online support forum for men in order to obtain a richer insight into their experience of infertility.

Methods

The data used in this study comprised all messages posted to the 'men's room' forum of an online infertility support community from January 2005 to June 2006. In total, 53 conversational threads were downloaded for analysis, yielding 728 individual messages. Each message included the date and time it was posted to the forums well as the unique sender name ($n = 166$).

Each message was analysed using an inductive thematic analysis approach with the guidelines set out by Braun & Clarke (2006). First of all, each message was read and re-read several times and any interesting features were coded. Next, each of the codes created were sorted into themes and all the data relevant to each theme was collated. After this, the data was systematically reviewed in order to make sure a name and a clear definition for each of the themes had been identified and that each of the themes sat comfortably with the coded extracts. The authors adopted an essentialist or realist framework, therefore were identified at the semantic level.

Findings

The analysis yielded five themes that reflected the male experience of infertility and included: 'Supporting dearest partner is our key role', 'Is this a good or bad pain?', 'Us blokes are mere spectators in most people's eyes', 'Sometimes a male perspective is needed' and 'I don't want to get my hopes up but I can't help it'.

Author reflections

The authors consider the online fertility support forum to be a novel but incredibly useful means through which to explore the experience of infertility from the 'silent' partner. They note the challenges involved in engaging men in research and suggest this approach offer unique and valuable insights.

Content communities: the example of YouTube

YouTube was founded in 2005 and is a video-sharing website that permits users to upload, view and share videos. The website includes a wide array of user-generated content that includes video clips, TV clips and music videos as well as amateur content such as video blogging, short original videos and educational videos. The vast majority of the content that has been uploaded to YouTube has been uploaded by individuals however some media corporations, for example the BBC, offer some of their material via this website. Those individuals who are not registered with YouTube can still watch videos but registration is required in order to upload an unlimited number of videos and most videos also allow users to post comments. Whilst YouTube is a globally successful website, it should be noted that not all countries permit YouTube to operate and have banned its use.

YouTube, as a research environment, has a number of potential applications and researchers may consider whether it may be a helpful platform through which to undertake research. Konijn *et al.*, (2013) provide a number of reasons as to why YouTube may be a useful environment through which to conduct research: (1) the popularity of YouTube, particularly among younger age groups (i.e. under 18s), may allow it to serve as an 'accommodating and convincing research setting for this age group' (p. 695); (2) it provides a viable means through which almost any kind of media content can be studied, such as commercials or pro-social content etc. In addition, different presentation formats are possible ranging from still images and text to audio visual materials and movies; (3) content can be easily edited and manipulated thereby making it suitable for controlled experimental designs; (4) the ability to post comments about the materials presented, that are publicly visible, makes it possible to explore 'peer influence'. In order to illustrate the potential application of YouTube as a research environment, Konijn *et al.*, (2013) present three scenarios illustrating how this website was used to conduct research. Given that each of these scenarios represents a fascinating insight into this novel research tool, a summary of each will be provided in Box 6.6.

BOX 6.6 Examples of YouTube as a research environment

Summary of research from Konijn, E.A. et al., (2013). YouTube as a research tool: three approaches. *CyberPsychology, Behavior & Social Networking*, 16(9), 695–701.

Approach 1: YouTube to create experimental materials and peer feedback Study materials were developed in YouTube in to explore how peer feedback on differently sized media models would impact upon adolescent girls' responses and body perceptions.

Background

The researchers noted the paradox that exists within the society with regards issues of body weight. That is, the media portray females who are thin as highly attractive and successful role models whilst obesity levels continue to rise. Furthermore, many studies have reported that adolescent girls are often negatively affected by the portrayal of the thin body ideal within the media. However, past research has demonstrated that accurately telling girls about the actual (under) weight of the displayed models could begin to negate this negative impact of media portrayal. The study described by the authors wished to consider the role of peer feedback as a strategy to counteract the impact of media portrayals. As a consequence, YouTube was considered useful as it allows users to post comments about the content being displayed and the researchers wished to harness this. Using theoretical reasoning, the researchers predicted that peers giving accurate weight information on very thin models would reduce negative body perceptions. Moreover, when peers included 'normal weight' information, girls may believe that the presented very thin model is considered of 'normal' shape, thereby, increasing negative body perceptions. Therefore, in order to explore causal effects, the researchers systematically combined media models ranging in body shape (i.e. extremely thin, thin, normal) with feedback from peers in terms of the weight of the model being displayed in YouTube. The variation stated the model to be either '6 kg underweight/ extremely thin,' '3 kg underweight/thin' or 'normal weight'.

How was YouTube used?

In order to create peer feedback, the team mimicked 'common' peer comments typical of responses to YouTube clips. These comments were manipulated in accordance with the experimental design (e.g. 'yes, for sure she is 6 kilos underweight'). This peer feedback was intended to provide feedback consistent with an adolescent's perspective. The materials used were digitally available media models and chosen to reflect the three body types required in the study design. Together, the media models and the online peer comments (i.e. 10 for each model) provided the experimental conditions. All this was included as an incorporated entity on YouTube and a screenshot of the full colour YouTube page (with all relevant content visible) was taken and included in an online questionnaire.

Findings

The results revealed that the peer feedback on the media modes influenced the effects of thin body ideals in the perceptions of the adolescent sample.

Reflections

The authors reflected on the use of YouTube and considered it to be an 'ecologically valid approach that worked well in our studies' (p. 696). They suggest that YouTube may be used in a range of research activities, particularly in the study of media effects in relation to peer feedback. They also note that YouTube is a popular tool with adolescents and is easy to use with regards the design of audio-visual materials to be used in controlled experiments.

Approach 2: YouTube as a measurement device
A measurement tool was developed in order to examine adolescents' preferences and responses to specific media content, using YouTube.

Background

Media content showing antisocial or risky behaviour can often be seen as popular by some young people therefore the authors argue there is a need to examine factors that may underpin adolescent preferences for antisocial, violent or risky media content.

How was YouTube used?

A new measure called the Media, Morals and Youth Questionnaire (MMaYQue) was developed using YouTube. In developing this questionnaire, a number of episodes of frequently portrayed media content on YouTube was drawn together. Popular clips were watched and rated in terms of portraying anti-social and pro-social behaviour using risk behaviour categories and the popularity of clips (e.g. number of hits, likings, reviews). Each clip was described in a handful of sentences and using these descriptions, the authors rated them on likeability and desire to view the clip in order to create a selection of attractive yet clearly distinguishable episodes of antisocial versus pro-social media content.

The initial MMaYQue questionnaire included 22 descriptions of popular YouTube clips. Of these, 14 were descriptions of anti-social behaviours (e.g. violence/aggression, sexual harassment/sexual exposure, substance abuse/binge drinking and reckless driving). The remaining 8 items were pro-social/neutral media content and used as filler items. The adolescents were asked to provide a range of ratings towards these descriptions.

The authors designed two formats for the MMaYQue with one including all content descriptions and formats as in the original YouTube layout, based on screenshots from YouTube clips. The results were then included as if they were the original YouTube clips in an online questionnaire. In the second, a more condensed format with fewer graphics was developed.

Findings

The analysis of responses by adolescents to the online questionnaire indicated that the MMaYQue had an acceptable internal structure and good criterion and discriminant validity.

Reflections

Again, the authors were satisfied with regards the role of YouTube and found it to be helpful in terms of being a tool to address their research question. They did suggest that future research should use more colourful content-related images, possibly even moving images, to further enhance the appeal to adolescents.

These examples suggest that YouTube may hold promise as a research environment and Konijn *et al.*, (2013) argue that YouTube made it possible to 'investigate systematically the combined influence of immediate peer feedback and a media model's weight status on adolescent girls' responses and body perceptions in experimental designs' (p. 700). Furthermore, they consider the graphical and textual nature of YouTube, as well as its 'plasticity' (p. 700), to be useful in terms of exerting control over both the media images and peer comments. They believe that YouTube has allowed researchers new ways to undertake experimental research into the *combined* influence of media and peers. In addition, the work ok Konijn *et al.*, (2013) does suggest that YouTube may be a useful means through which to undertake research on message processing. For example, they suggest that variations in expert and peer senders of information could be studied or different subcultures (i.e. through manipulating the language and use of specific nicknames).

Researchers may also wish to consider the value of engaging with an ecologically valid research environment. The presentation of media content may be attractive to specific age groups, through YouTube, and this could be harnessed by researchers.

Virtual second worlds: the example of Second Life

In recent years, there has been a growing interest in virtual worlds. Virtual worlds are online 'worlds' where nearly every aspect of human endeavours and actions can be undertaken virtually. Using avatars, individuals can engage with their virtual environment with their own designed and customized character. To psychologists, virtual worlds represent unique opportunities to explore online behaviour (e.g. does online behaviour impact on offline behaviour) but also as a virtual space through which to conduct research.

One popular virtual world is Second Life (www.secondlife.com) that uses avatars to navigate the 3D digital world and interact with other avatars online in real time, using either speech or text to do so. While some authors would argue that the popularity of Second Life has reached its peak, nevertheless, it represents a fascinating example of such a virtual world and may be of interest to those unfamiliar with second worlds online.

Jarrett (2009) discusses some fascinating examples of psychological research being conducted on those individuals who engage in the Second Life virtual world. Indeed, it is argued that there is considerable evidence to suggest that the ways in which individuals interact in Second Life mirrors the ways in which they interact in the offline, physical world. What this means for researchers is that there exists the possibility of undertaking large scale studies exploring social issues that have meaning in the real world. Indeed, through Second Life projects may take place that otherwise might not have on account of their complexity and/or expense.

Online software packages

As we have seen in previous chapters, there are different software packages out there that may be helpful to researchers. These packages vary in the level of functionality and of course the price but the good news is that there are some free packages that can help those researchers on a budget. Here are some suggestions to get you

Table 6.2   Selected software packages

Company	Web address	Pricing
Topsy	http://www.topsy.com	Free (Search and analyse tweets, videos, photos and influencers)
Rapidminer	http://www.rapidminer.com	Free trial available (open source system for data and text mining)
Technorati	http://www.technorati.com	Free (An internet search engine for searching blogs)

started but it is worth having a look to see what other packages exist as new companies and programmes launch all the time (Table 6.2).

Chapter summary

In this chapter, we have considered the social media landscape as a research environment. Indeed, such a landscape is constantly evolving as new examples of social media continue to appear on an almost daily basis. However, to aid our understanding of social media a classification system was described that considers social media along two complimentary set of processes: social presence/media richness and self-presentation/self-disclosure. Such a classification system will help those unfamiliar with social media to consider which if any of these processes are important with regards their use of social media for research purposes. From this, we considered a range of examples of both research about social media as well as research using social media. Regardless of individuals' views towards social media, it is something that is here to stay and for psychologists the opportunities for research are plentiful.

Further reading

Boyd, D.M. & Ellison, N.B. (2008). Social network sites: definition, history and scholarship. *Journal of Computer-Mediated Communication*, 13, 210–230.

Chew, C. & Eysenbach, G. (2010). Pandemics in the age of Twitter: content analysis of Tweets during the 2009 H1N1 outbreak. *PloS One*, 5(11), e14118.

Hookway, N. (2008). 'Entering the blogosphere': some strategies for using blogs in social research. *Qualitative Research*, 8, 91–113.

Jarrett, C. (2009). Get a second life. *The Psychologist*, 22(6), 490–493.

Konijn, E.A., Veldhuis, J. & Plaisier, X.S. (2013). YouTube as a research tool: three approaches. *CyberPsychology, Behavior & Social Networking*, 16(9), 695–701.

Leng, H.K. (2013). Methodological issues in using data from social networking sites. *CyberPsychology, Behavior & Social Networking*, 16(9), 686–689.

Moreno, M.A., Goniu, N., Moreno, P.S. & Diekema, D. (2013). Ethics of social media research: common concerns and practical considerations. *CyberPsychology, Behaviour & Social Networking*, 16(9), 708–713.

Appendix A: Participant Information Page – Online Survey Example

I would like to invite you to take part in my research study. Before you decide whether or not to participate, it is important for you to understand the purpose of the research and what it will involve. Please take time to read the following information carefully. If you feel that any part of the study is not entirely clear or if you would like more information prior to participation, then please do not hesitate to contact me (contact details below).

What is the purpose of the study?

I am interested in exploring the experiences of people like you who participate in **XXXXXXXXX** disease online discussion forums. In particular, I wish to learn about your experiences of using the forum and what you liked and didn't like about it as well as trying to understand what role, if any, it may have in helping people just like you. Participation is entirely voluntary.

This study is funded by **XXXXXXXXXXXXXXXXXXXXX**.

Why have I been invited?

You have been invited to participate in this study as you currently access a **XXXXXXXXX** disease online discussion forum, or have done so in the past. I am interested in exploring your experiences, regardless of whether you access these forums a little or a lot. All views and experiences are valid and helpful to learn more about the issue.

How long is the study?

The study will take around 10–30 minutes.

Do I have to take part?

Your participation in this study is entirely voluntary. If you agree to take part, we will ask you to complete an online consent form. You are free to withdraw from the study at any time without giving a reason, though should you wish to do so, we recommend doing this within 7 days of completing the online survey. After that point, it may not be possible to remove your data from the study, which means that it may still be used in our analysis. However, if you have any questions about this, please feel free to contact us.

What will I be asked to do if I take part?

If you agree to take part, you will be invited to answer some questions about your experiences with the online discussion forum. These questions will be a mixture of 'tick box' style and open-ended questions. As I am particularly interested in hearing about your experiences – your own thoughts and views are very important – I have included several open-ended questions, so you can tell me what you think in your own words.

What are the possible disadvantages and risks of taking part?

The survey only deals with topics you would expect to see being discussed in the online forum and should not be distressing to you. While the likelihood of the survey causing distress is extremely small, I will be able to provide support to participants, if such a situation arises (i.e. useful information). As an online participant in this research, there is always the (very small) risk of intrusion by outside agents, that is, hacking, and therefore the possibility of being identified.

How will I benefit from participating in this study?

If you are kind enough to participate in this study by completing the online survey then, if you wish, your name will be included in a prize draw (1st prize is an online shopping voucher for £50; 2nd prize is £30). In order to do this, I would need you to provide a contact email address so that if you win, I can send you an electronic voucher. However, this is entirely optional and if you prefer not to leave your name that is fine. In any event, your participation will provide a great deal of insight into how such forums are supporting people like yourself and how they can be developed going forward.

If I need to speak to someone about the research, whom should I contact?

If you have any questions, queries or concerns regarding the study, please contact the Principal Investigator using the contact details below.

What will happen if I don't want to carry on with the study?

Your participation in this study is entirely voluntary. You are free to withdraw from the study at any time without giving a reason by clicking the 'exit study' button located on each question page.

How will we use the results of this research?

The results will be used to help improve XXXXXXXX online forums through scientific journal papers and other dissemination activities such as conferences etc. as well as feeding back our findings to the forums that participated.

Am I able to know the results of the study?

Yes, if you would like a summary of the results, please contact the researcher (details below).
    Contact details:

Appendix B: Consent – Online Survey Example

I confirm that I have read and understood the information regarding the above study and have the relevant information to contact the researcher to ask any questions.

1. I understand that my participation is voluntary and that I am free to withdraw at any time, without giving any reason. I understand that should I withdraw after 7 days post submission then the information collected so far cannot be erased and that this information may still be used in the study analysis.
2. I understand that my personal details will be kept confidential.
3. I understand that I will be asked to complete some questions and that the data from these will be used to understand how online support forums may help individuals living with this condition and may be used in journal papers and conference presentations.
4. I understand that my data from this study will be anonymized and that only members of the research team will have access to the data and my personal information.
5. I agree to take part in the above study.

Appendix C: Debrief and Thank You

I would like to extend my huge thanks for taking the time to complete this online survey. This work has been funded by the **XXXXXXXXXXX**, UK and will be invaluable in helping understand how such forums support individuals just like you and what can be done to further improve them.

If you have any questions about the research please contact the Principal Investigator:

Glossary

AIM   AOL instant messenger.

ARPANET   the Advanced Research Projects Agency Network was one of the world's first operational packet switching networks, it was the first network to implement TCP/IP.

Asynchronous communication   interaction that is not occurring at the same time between sender and receiver.

Attachment   a computer file (e.g. pdf) sent along with an email.

Bandwith   measurement of bit-rate of available or consumed data communication resources expressed in bits per second or multiples of it (e.g. 56 kbits/s).

BITNET   short form of Because It's Time NETwork and is a network of academic sites.

Blog   a blog is short for "web log" and is a web page that includes a range of items posted to it, such as stories, articles, diary entries, photos. Blogs are a popular medium for communication professional, political, news, trendy and other specialized web communities. Blogs may include RSS feeds, which allow an individual to subscribe and receive regular alerts of new content on specific blogs.

Browser   a software application that is used for retrieving, presenting and traversing information resources on the World Wide Web.

BUDDY LIST   a list of people to keep track of, commonly used in instant messaging applications.

Bulletin-board   a surface intended for the posting of public messages. In the online context, a bulletin board is often referred to as a message board or online discussion forum.

Chat room   a form of synchronous conferencing or discussion facility online. The ability to enter into discussions with multiple people in the chat room differentiates this from instant messaging programmes that are usually designed for one to one communication.

Computer-mediated communication   any communication transaction that takes place through the use of two or more electronic devices. Whilst the term has typically been used in the context of computer-mediated formats, such as chat rooms, email or instant messaging, it has also been applied to other formats, such as text messaging.

Cookies a small amount of data sent from a website and stored in a user's web browser while the user is browsing that website. Each time the user then loads the website, the browser sends the cookie back to the server to notify website of the user's previous activity.

Cyberspace a metaphor that describes the non-physical terrain created by computer systems and the flow of data through the network of interconnected computers.

Discussion thread messages grouped together in a hierarchy by topic, with any replies to a message grouped together near to the original message.

Distribution list a feature of an email programme that allows users to maintain a list of mail addresses and send messages to all of them at once.

Download copying something from a primary source to a more peripheral one, such as saving something retrieved from the web to the desktop or USB.

Emoticons a pictorial representation of a facial expression and helps convey a person's mood or feelings.

Encryption is the process of encoding messages (or information) in such a way that online selected authorized individuals can read it.

End user license agreement the contract between the licensor and purchaser or user that establishes their right to use specific software.

Firewall a software or hardware-based network security system that controls the incoming and outgoing network traffic by analyzing the data packets and determining whether they should be allowed through or not, based on specific rules set.

Flaming also known as bashing, is hostile and insulting interaction between Internet users online, usually as the result of heated argument or debate.

Gatekeeper a person who controls access to something.

HTML hypertext markup language is the authoring language used to create used to create documents on the World Wide Web.

ICQ an instant messaging programme.

Internet service provider is a business or organization that offers users access to the Internet.

IP address an internet protocol address is a numerical label assigned to each device (e.g. personal computer) participating in a network that uses the internet protocol for communication.

Login the credentials required to access a computer system.

Meta-analysis a statistical technique that focuses on contrasting and combining results from across different studies in order to identify patterns across study results, sources of disagreement across results or other interesting relationships that may come to light in the context of multiple studies.

Microblog a form of blogging that allows users to write brief text updates (usually less than 200 characters) and publish them, either to be viewed by anyone or by a restricted group that is chosen by the user.

MMO a massively multiplayer online game (also called MMOG) that is capable of supporting many players simultaneously.

Moderator a person given special authority to monitor and enforce the rules of an online discussion forum.

MUD a multi-user dungeon (also known as multi-user domain), is a multi-player real-time virtual world.

Netiquette a set of social conventions that help facilitate interactions over networks.

Pin a personal identification number used to authenticate a user to a system.

Posts a message uploaded by an individual to a discussion forum.

Probability a measure or estimation of the likelihood that an event will occur.

Proxy an intermediary server (or application).

Radio button also known as an option button, is a graphical user interface element that allows the user to select one of a predetermined set of options.

Router a device that forwards data packets between computer networks.

Sampling frame a list of all those within a population that may be sampled.

Scroll to slide text, videos or images across a computer display.

Search engine a software system that is designed to search for information on the World Wide Web.

Social desirability is the tendency to respond in a way that is deemed more desirable by others than their 'true' answer. This is done to project a favourable image of themselves and to avoid receiving negative evaluations.

Social networking service is a platform to build social networks or social relations between people.

Software any set of machine readable instructions that directs a computer's processor to perform specific operations.

Spam is the use of electronic messaging systems to send unsolicited bulk messages, often advertising, indiscriminately.

Spreadsheet is an interactive computer application for the organization and analysis of data in a tabular format.

Synchronous communication is the interaction occurring at the same time between the sender and receiver (and vice versa).

TCP/IP is a networking model and a set of communications protocols used for the Internet.

Transcription is the conversation of speech into a written or textual document.

URL is a uniform resource locator (also known as a web address) is a specific character string that constitutes a reference to a resource.

Usenet is a worldwide distributed Internet discussion system. Users read and post messages to one or more categories, known as newsgroups.

Username is the account name for a user used to gain access to a computer or application.

Verbatim means in exactly the same words as was used previously.

References

Anderson, B., Fagan, P., Woodnutt, T. *et al.* (2012). Facebook psychology: popular questions answered by research. *Psychology of Popular Media Culture,* 1(1), 23–37.

Association of Internet Researchers (2012). Ethical decision making and internet research. http://aoir.org/reports/ethics2.pdf

Ayling, R. & Mewse, A.J. (2009). Evaluating Internet interviews with gay men. *Qualitative Health Research,* 19, 566–576.

Bargh, J. A. & McKenna, K. Y. (2004). The Internet and social life. *Annual Review of Psychology,* 55, 573–590.

Beck, C.T. (2005). Benefits of participating in Internet interviews: women helping women. *Qualitative Health Research,* 15, 411–422.

Benfield, J.A. & Szlemko, W.J. (2006). Internet-based data collection: promises and realities. *Journal of Research Practice,* 2(2), Article D1.

Biesenbach-Lucas, S. & Weasenforth, D. (2002). Virtual office hours: negotiation strategies in electronic conferencing. *Computer Assisted Language Learning,* 15, 147–165.

Birnbaum, M.H. (2004). Human research and data collection via the Internet. *Annual Review of Psychology,* 55, 803–832.

Blanchard, A.L. (2004). Virtual behavior settings: an application of behavior settings theories to virtual communities. *Journal of Computer-Mediated Communication,* 9(2). http://jcmc.indiana.edu/vol9/issue2/blanchard.htmlBlood, R. (2002). Weblogs: a history and perspective. In Rodzvilla, J. (ed.). *We've Got Blog: How Weblogs Are Changing Our Culture.* Cambridge, MA: Perseus.

Bosnjak, M., Neubarth, W., Couper, M.P., Bandilla, W. & Kaczmire, L. (2008). Prenotification in web-based access panel surveys: the influence of mobile text messaging versus email on response rates and sample composition. *Social Science Computer Review,* 26, 213–223.

Bowker, N. & Tuffin, K. (2004). Using the online medium for discursive research about people with disabilities. *Social Science Computer Review,* 22(2), 228–241.

Boyd, D.M. & Ellison, N.B. (2008). Social network sites: definition, history and scholarship. *Journal of Computer-Mediated Communication,* 13, 210–230.

Brandtzæg, P.B., Heim, J., & Karahasanović, A. (2011). Understanding the new digital divide—a typology of Internet users in Europe. *International Journal of Human-Computer Studies, 69*(3), 123–138.

Braun, V. & Clarke, C. (2006). Using thematic analysis in Psychology. *Qualitative Research in Psychology, 3*(2), 77–101.

British Psychological Society (2009). *Code of ethics and conduct.* Leicester, UK: British Psychological Society.

British Psychological Society (2010). *Code of human research ethics.* Leicester, UK: British Psychological Society.

British Psychological Society (2013). *Ethics guidelines for Internet-mediated research.* Leicester, UK: British Psychological Society.

Broderick, J.E. (2008). Electronic diaries: appraisal and current status. *Pharmaceutical Medicine, 22,* 69.

Bruckman, A. (1999). The day after net day: approaches to educational use of the Internet. *Convergence, 51*(1), 24–46.

Boyd, D. (2006). Friends, Friendsters, and MySpace Top 8: writing community into being on social network sites. *First Monday,* 11(12). Retrieved 30 January 2015 from http:// www.firstmonday.org/issues/issue11_12/boyd/

Buchanan, H. & Coulson, N.S. (2007). Accessing dental anxiety online support groups: An exploratory qualitative study of motives and experiences. *Patient Education & Counseling, 66*(3), 263–269.

Butler, B.S. (2001). Membership size, communication activity and sustainability: a resource based model of online social structures. *Information Systems Research, 12*(4), 346–362.

Chen, P. & Hinton, S.M. (1999). Real time interviewing using the world wide web. *Sociological Research Online, 4,* 3.

Chew, C. & Eysenbach, G. (2010). Pandemics in the age of Twitter: content analysis of Tweets during the 2009 H1N1 outbreak. *PloS One,* 5(11), e14118.

Cook, C., Heath, F. & Thompson, R.L. (2000). A meta-analysis of response rates in web- or Internet-based surveys. *Educational and Psychological Measurement, 60,* 821–836.

Couch, D. & Liamputtong, P. (2008). Online dating and mating: the use of the Internet to find sexual partners. *Qualitative Health Research,* 18(2), 268–279.

Coulson, N.S. (2013). How do online patient support communities affect the experience of Inflammatory Bowel Disease? An online survey. *Journal of the Royal Society of Medicine Short Reports, 4*(8), 1–8.

Couper, M.P. (2000). Web surveys: a review of issues and approaches. *Public Opinion Quarterly, 64,* 464–494.

Couper, M.P., Kapteyn, A., Schonlau, M. & Winter, J. (2007). Noncoverage and nonresponse in an Internet survey. *Social Science Research*, 36, 131–148.

Couper, M.P., Tourangeau, R., Conrad, F.G. & Crawford, S.D. (2004). What they see is what we get – response options for web surveys. *Social Science Computer Review*, 22, 111–127.

Crawford, S.D. (2006). *Web survey implementation.* University of North Carolina.

Crawford, S.D., Couper, M.P. & Lamias, M.J. (2001). Web surveys: perceptions of burden. *Social Science Computer Review*, 19, 146–162.

Crocker, J. & Major, B. (1989). Social stigma and self-esteem: the self-protective properties of stigma. *Psychological Review*, 96(4), 608–630.

Curasi, C.F. (2001). A critical exploration of face-to-face interviewing vs. computer-mediated interviewing. *International Journal of Market Research*, 43(4), 361–375.

Cutrona, C.E. & Suhr, J. (1992). Controllability of stressful events and satisfaction with spouse support behaviours. *Communication Research*, 19, 154–174.

Daft, R.L. & Lengel, R.H. (1986). Organizational information requirements, media richness, and structural design. *Management Science*, 32(5), 554–571.

Davis, M., Bolding, G., Hart, G., Sheer, L. & Elford, J. (2004). Reflecting on the experience of interviewing online: perspectives from the Internet and HIV study in London. *AIDS Care*, 16(8), 944–952.

Di Fraia, G. (2004). *E-Research.* Laterza, Italy: Bari.

Dickerson, S.S. & Feitshans, L.A. (2003). Internet users becoming immersed in the virtual world: implications for nurses. *CIN: Computers, Informatics, Nursing*, 21(6), 300–308.

Dillman, D.A. (2000). *Mail and Internet surveys: the tailored design method.* New York: John Wiley & Sons.

Dillman, D.A., Tortora, R., Conradt, J. & Bowker, D. (1998). Influence of plain vs. fancy design on response rates for web surveys. Paper presented at the Joint Statistical Meetings, Dallas, Texas.

Diment, K. & Garrett-Jones, S. (2007). How demographic characteristics affect mode preference in a postal/web mixed-mode survey of Australian researchers. *Social Science Computer Review*, 25, 510–517.

Dix, K.L. & Anderson, J. (2000). Distance no longer a barrier: using the Internet as a survey tool in educational research. *International Education Journal*, 2(1), 3–9.

Dommeyer, C.J. & Moriarty, E. (2000). Comparing two forms of an e-mail survey: embedded vs. attached. *International Journal of Market Research*, 42(1), 39–50.

Duggleby, W. (2000). What about focus group interaction data? *Qualitative Health Research*, 15(6), 832–840.

Edwards, P., Roberts, I., Clarke, M., DiGuiseppi, C., Pratap, S., Wentz, R. et al. (2002). Increasing response rates to postal questionnaires: systematic review. *British Medical Journal*, 324.

Egan, J., Chenoweth, L. & McAuliffe, D. (2006). Email-facilitated qualitative interviews with traumatic brain injury survivors: a new and accessible method. *Brain Injury*, 20(12), 1283–1294.

Evans, J.R. & Mathur, A. (2005). The value of online surveys. *Internet Research*, 15(2), 195–219.

Eysenbach, G. (2004). Improving the quality of web surveys: the checklist for reporting results of Internet e-surveys (CHERRIES). *Journal of Medical Internet Research*, 6(3), e34.

Fan, W. & Yan, Z. (2010). Factors affecting response rates of the web survey: a systematic review. *Computers in Human Behavior*, 26, 132–139.

Fawcett, J. & Buhle, E.L. (1995). Using the Internet for data collection: an innovative electronic strategy. *Computers in Nursing*, 13, 273–279.

Fox, F.E., Morris, M. & Rumsey, N. (2007). Doing synchronous online focus groups with young people: methodological reflections. *Qualitative Health Research*, 17(4), 539–547.

Gangadharbatla, H. (2008). Facebook me: collective self-esteem, need to belong, and Internet self-efficacy as predictors of the iGeneration's attitudes toward social networking sites. *Journal of Interactive Advertising*, 8, 1–28.

Goffman, E. (1959). *The presentation of self in everyday life*. New York: Doubleday Anchor Books.

Golder, S.A., Wilkinson, D.M. & Huberman, B.A. (2007). Rhythms of social interaction: messaging within a massive online network. *Communities & Technologies*, 41–66.

Goritz, A.S. (2006). Incentives in web studies: methodological issues and a review. *International Journal of Internet Science*, 1, 58–70.

Granello, D.H. & Wheaton, J.E. (2004). Online data collection: strategies for research. *Journal of Counseling & Development*, 82(4), 387–393.

Griffiths, M. (2010). The use of online methodologies in data collection for gambling and gaming addictions. *International Journal of Mental Health and Addiction*, 8, 8–20.

Groves, R.M., Cialdini, R.B. & Couper, M.P. (1992). Understanding the decision to participate in a survey. *Public Opinion Quarterly*, 56, 475–495.

Hamilton, R.J. & Bowers, B.J. (2006). Internet recruitment and email interviews in qualitative studies. *Qualitative Health Research*, 16(6), 821–835.

Hargittai, E. (2008). Whose space? Differences among users and non-users of social network sites. *Journal of Computer-Mediated Communication*, 13, 276–297.

Haythornthwaite, C. (2005). Social networks and Internet connectivity effects. *Information, Communication & Society*, 8(2), 125–147.

Heerwegh, D. & Loosveldt, G. (2002). Web surveys: the effect of controlling survey access using PIN numbers. *Social Science Computer Review*, 20, 10–21.

Heerwegh, D. & Loosveldt, G. (2003). An evaluation of the semiautomatic login procedure to control web survey access. *Social Science Computer Review*, 21, 223–234.

Heerwegh, D., Vanhove, T., Matthijs, K. & Loosveldt, G. (2005). The effects of personalization on response rates and data quality in web surveys. *International Journal of Social Research Methodology: Theory and Practice*, 18, 85–99.

Hennekam, R.C. (2011). Care for patients with ultra-rare disorders. *European Journal of Medical Genetics*, 54(3), 220–224.

Hewson, C. (2003). *Internet research methods: a practical guide for the social and behavioural sciences*. London, UK: Sage.

Hewson, C., Laurent, D. & Vogel, C. (1996). Proper methodologies for psychological and sociological studies conducted via the Internet. *Behavior Research Methods*, 28(2), 186–191.

Hinchcliffe, V. & Gavin, H. (2009). Social and virtual networks: evaluating synchronous online interviewing using instant messenger. *The Qualitative Report*, 14(2), 318–340.

Holtz, P., Kronberger, N. & Wagner, W. (2012). Analyzing Internet forums. *Journal of Media Psychology*, 24(2), 55–66.

Hookway, N. (2008). 'Entering the blogosphere': some strategies for using blogs in social research. *Qualitative Research*, 8, 91–113.

Hunt, N. & McHale, S. (2007). A practical guide to the e-mail interview. *Qualitative Health Research*, 17, 1415–1421.

Internet World Stats (2013). http://www.internetworldstats.com/stats.htm. Retrieved 24 March 2014.

James, N. & Busher, H. (2009). *Online interviewing*. London, UK: Sage.

Jarrett, C. (2009). Get a second life. *The Psychologist*, 22(6), 490–493.

Joinson, A. (1999). Social desirability, anonymity, and Internet-based questionnaires. *Behavior Research Methods, Instruments, & Computers*, 31(3), 433–438.

Joinson, A. (2003). *Understanding the psychology of Internet behaviour: virtual worlds, real lives*. Basingstoke, UK: Palgrave Macmillan.

Jowett, A. & Peel, E. (2009). Chronic illness in non-heterosexual contexts: an online survey. *Feminism & Psychology*, 19(4), 454–474.

Jowett, A., Peel, E. & Shaw, R. (2011). Online interviewing in psychology: reflections on the process. *Qualitative Research in Psychology*, 8(4), 354–369.

Kaplan, A.M. & Haenlein, M. (2010). Users of the world, unite! The challenges and opportunities of social media. *Business Horizons*, 53, 59–68.

Karchner, R.A. (2001). The journey ahead: thirteen teachers report how the Internet influences literacy instruction in their K-12 classrooms. *Reading Research Quarterly*, 36(4), 442–466.

Kim, B.S.K., Brenner, B.R., Liang, C.T.H., & Asay, P.A. (2003). A qualitative study of adaptation experiences of 1.5-generation Asian Americans. *Cultural Diversity & Ethnic Minority Psychology*, 9(2), 156–170.

Kitchin, R. (1998). *Cyberspace: the world in the wires*. Chichester, UK: Wiley.

Konijn, E.A., Veldhuis, J. & Plaisier, X.S. (2013). YouTube as a research tool: three approaches. *CyberPsychology, Behavior & Social Networking*, 16(9), 695–701.

Krantz, J.H., Ballard, J. & Scher, J. (1997). Comparing the results of laboratory and World Wide Web samples on the determinants of female attractiveness. *Behavioral Research Methods, Instruments, & Computers*, 29, 264–269.

Kraut, R., Kiesler, S., Boneva, B., Cummings, J., Helgeson, V. & Crawford, A. (2002). The Internet paradox revisited. *Journal of Social Issues*, 58, 49–74.

Kraut, R., Olson, J., Banaji, M., Bruckman, A., Cohen, J. & Couper, N. (2004). Psychological research online: report of the Board of Scientific Affairs' Advisory Group on the conduct of research on the Internet. *American Psychologist*, 59(2), 105–117.

Kraut, R., Patterson, M., Lundmark, V., Kiesler, S., Mukopadhyay, T. & Scherlis, W. (1998). Internet paradox: a social technology that reduces social involvement and psychological well-being. *American Psychologist*, 53, 1017–1031.

Krieck, M., Dreesman, J., Otrusina, L., & Denecke, K. (2011). A new age of public health: identifying disease outbreaks by analyzing tweets. In *Proceedings of Health Web-Science Workshop, ACM Web Science Conference*.

Krueger, R.A. (1994). *Focus groups: a practical guide for applied research* (2nd Ed.). Thousand Oaks, CA: Sage.

Kvale, S. (1983). The qualitative research interview: a phenomenological and hermeneutical mode of understanding. *Journal of Phenomenological Psychology*, 14, 171–196.

Leng, H.K. (2013). Methodological issues in using data from social networking sites. *CyberPsychology, Behavior & Social Networking*, 16(9), 686–689.

MacElroy, B. (2000). Measuring response rates in online surveys. *Quirk's Marketing Research Review*, 14(4), 50–52.

Manfreda, K.L., Batagelj, Z. & Vehovar, V. (2002). Design of web survey questionnaires: three basic experiments. *Journal of Computer-Mediated Communication*, 7(3).

McKenna, K.Y.A. & Bargh, J.A. (1998). Coming out in the age of the Internet: identity "demarginalization" through virtual group participation. *Journal of Personality & Social Psychology*, 75, 681–694.

Malik, S.H. & Coulson, N.S. (2008a). Computer-mediated infertility support groups: an exploratory study of online experiences. *Patient Education & Counseling*, 73(1), 105–113.

Malik, S.H. & Coulson, N.S. (2008b). The male experience of infertility: A thematic analysis of an online infertility support group bulletin board. *Journal of Reproductive and Infant Psychology*, 26(1), 18–30.

Malik, S.H. & Coulson, N.S. (2010a). Coping with infertility online: an examination of self-help mechanisms in an infertility online support group. *Patient Education & Counseling*, 81, 315–318.

Malik, S.H. & Coulson, N.S. (2010b). 'They all supported me but I felt like I suddenly didn't belong anymore': an exploration of perceived disadvantages to online support seeking. *Journal of Psychosomatic Obstetrics & Gynecology*, 31(3), 140–149.

Malik, S. & Coulson, N.S. (2011). The therapeutic potential of the Internet: exploring self-help processes in an Internet forum for young people with Inflammatory Bowel Disease. *Gastroentereology Nursing*, 34(6), 439–448.

Manfreda, K.L., Bosniak, M., Berzelak, J., Haas, I., & Vehovar, V. (2008). Web surveys versus other survey modes – A meta-analysis comparing response rates. *International Journal of Market Research*, 50(1), 79–104.

Mann, C. & Stewart, F. (2000). *Internet communication in qualitative research: a handbook for researching online*. London, UK: Sage.

Meho, L.I. (2006). E-mail interviewing in qualitative research: a methodological discussion. *Journal of the American Society for Information Science and Technology*, 57(10), 1284–1295.

Merton, R.K. (1987). The focussed interview and focus groups: continuities and discontinuities. *The Public Opinion Quarterly*, 51(4), 550–566.

Milgram, S. (1977). *The individual in the social world*. New York: McGraw Hill.

Moreno, M.A., Goniu, N., Moreno, P.S. & Diekema, D. (2013). Ethics of social media research: common concerns and practical considerations. *CyberPsychology, Behaviour & Social Networking*, 16(9), 708–713.

Murray, C.D. (2004). An interpretative phenomenological analysis of the embodiment of artficial limbs. *Disability and Rehabilitation*, 26(16), 963–973.

Murray, C.D. & Sixsmith, J. (1998). E-mail: a qualitative research medium for interviewing? *International Journal of Social Research Methodology*, 1(2), 103–121.

Murray, P.J. (1997). Using focus groups in qualitative research. *Qualitative Health Research*, 7(4), 542–549.

Nardi, B.A., Schiano, D.J., Gumbrecht, M. & Swartz, L. (2004). Why we Blog. *Communications of the ACM*, 47(12), 41–46.

Nichols, A.L., & Maner, J.K. (2008). The good-subject effect: investigating participant demand characteristics. *Journal of General Psychology*, 135(2), 151–165.

Nosek, B.A., Banaji, M.R., & Greenwald, A.G. (2002). E-research: ethics, security, design, and control in psychological research on the Internet. *Journal of Social Issues*, 58(1), 161–176.

Office for National Statistics (2014). Internet access – households and individuals. *Statistical Bulletin*, August, 1–50.

Oringderff, J. (2004). "My way": piloting an online focus group. *International Journal of Qualitative Methods*, 3(3), 69–75.

Orne, M.T. (1962). On the social-psychology of the psychological experiment: with particular reference to demand characteristics and their implications. *American Psychologist*, 17(11), 776–783.

Panteli, N. (2002). Richness, power cues and email text. *Information & Management*, 40(2), 75–86.

Paterson, B. & Scott-Findley, S. (2002). Critical issues in interviewing people with traumatic brain injury. *Qualitative Health Research*, 12, 399–409.

Peacock, S., Robertson, A., Williams, S. & Clausen, M.G. (2009). The role of learning technoligists in supporting e-research. *ALT-J, Research in Learning Technology*, 17(2), 115–129.

Peluchette, J. & Karl, K. (2008). Social networking profiles: an examination of student attitudes regarding use and appropriateness of content. *CyberPsychology & Behavior*, 11, 95–97.

Pennebaker, J.W. (1993). Putting stress into words: health, linguistic and therapeutic implications. *Behavior Research & Therapy*, 31(6), 539–548.

Peytchev, A., Couper, M.P., McCabe, S.E. & Crawford, S.D. (2006). Web survey design: paging verus scrolling. *Public Opinion Quarterly*, 70(4), 596–607.

Piper, A.I. (1998). Conducting social science laboratory experiments on the World Wide Web. *Library & Information Science Research*, 20(1), 5–21.

Porter, S.R. & Whitcomb, M.E. (2003). The impact of contact type on web survey response rates. *Public Opinion Quarterly, 67*, 579–588.

Prandy, S.L., Norris, D., Lester, J. & Hoch, D.B. (2001). Expanding the guidelines for electronic communication with patients: application to a specific tool. *Journal of the American Medical Informatics Association*, 8(4), 344–348.

Reips, U.-D. (2000). The web experiment method: advantages, disadvantages and solutions. In M.H. Birnbaum (Ed.) *Psychology Experiments on the Internet* (pp. 89–117). San Diego, CA: Academic Press.

Rentfrow, P.J. & Gosling, S.D. (2003). The do re mis of everyday life: examining the structure and personality of correlates of music preferences. *Journal of Personality & Social Psychology, 81*, 1236–1256.

Rogelberg, S.G., Conway, J.M., Sederburg, M.E., Spitzmüller, C., Aziz, S. & Knight, W.E. (2003). Profiling active and passive nonrespondents to an organizational survey. *Journal of Applied Psychology, 88*, 1104–1114.

Rosenthal, R. (1966). *Experimenter Effects in Behavioral Research*. New York: Appleton-Century-Crofts.

Rosser, B.R.S., Miner, M.H., Bockting, W.O. et al., (2009). HIV Risk and the Internet: Results of the Men's INTernet Sex (MINTS) Study. *AIDS and Behavior, 13*(4), 746–756.

Rui, J.R., Chen, Y. & Damiano, A. (2013). Health organizations providing and seeking social support: a twitter-based content analysis. *CyberPsychology, Behavior & Social Networking, 16* (9), 669–673.

Schroeder, R. (1997). Networked worlds: social aspects of multi-user virtual reality. *Sociological Research Online, 2*(4).

Schultz, D.P. (1972). The human subject in psychological research. In C.L. Sheridan (Ed.), *Readings for Experimental Psychology* (pp. 263–282). New York: Holt.

Sears, D.O. (1986). College sophomores in the laboratory: influences of a narrow data base on social psychology's view of human nature. *Journal of Personality and Social Psychology, 51*(3), 515.

Shea, V. (1994). *Netiquette*. San Fransisco, CA: Albion Books.

Sheehan, K.B. & McMillan, S.J. (1999). Response variation in email surveys: an exploration. *Journal of Advertising Research, 39*, 45–54.

Shih, T.-H. & Fan, X. (2009). Comparing response rates in e-mail and paper surveys: a meta-analysis. *Educational Research Review, 4*(1), 26–40.

Shobat, M. & Musch, J. (2003). Online auctions as a research tool: a field experiment on ethnic discrimination. *Swiss Journal of Social Psychology, 62*, 139–145.

Short, J., Williams, E. & Christie, B. (1976). *The social psychology of telecommunications*. Hoboken, NJ: John Wiley & Sons Ltd.

Sintjago, A. & Link, A. (2012). From synchronous to asynchronous: researching online focus groups. In Duin, A.H., Nater, E. &. Anklesaria, F. (eds). *Cultivating change in the academy: 50+ stories from the digital frontlines at the University of Minnesota in 2012*. Retrieved from http://purl.umn.edu/125273

Skitka, L.J. & Sargis, E.G. (2006). The Internet as psychological laboratory. *Annual Review of Psychology, 57*, 529–555.

Smart, R. (1966). Subject selection bias in psychological research. *Canadian Psychologist, 7a*, 115–121.

Smith, M. A. & Leigh, B. (1997). Virtual subjects: using the Internet as an alternative source of subjects and research environment. *Behavior Research Methods, Instruments, & Computers, 29*(4), 496–505.

Smith, J.A., Flowers, P. & Larkin, M. (2009). *Interpretative phenomenological analysis*. London: Sage.

Srivastava, S., John, O.P., Gosling, S.D. & Potter, J. (2003). Development of personality in adulthood: set like plaster or persistent change? *Journal of Personality & Social Psychology, 84*, 1041–1053.

Stewart, K. & Williams, M. (2005). Researching online populations: the use of online focus groups for social research. *Qualitative Research, 5*(4), 395–416.

Stieger, S. & Göritz, A.S. (2006). Using instant messaging for Internet-based interviews. *CyberPsychology & Behavior, 9*(5), 552–559.

Suler, J. (2004). The online disinhibition effect. *CyberPsychology & Behavior, 7*(3), 321–326.

Suzuki, L.K. & Calzo, J.P. (2004). The search for peer advice in cyberspace: an examination of online teen bulletin boards about health and sexuality. *Journal of Applied Developmental Psychology, 25*(6), 685–698.

Tates, K., Zwaanswijk, M., Otten, R., van Dulmen, S., Hoogerbrugge, P.M., Kamps, W.A. & Bensing, J.M. (2009). Online focus groups as a tool to collect data in hard-to-include populations: examples from paediatric oncology. *BMC Medical Research Methodology, 9*(15).

Thelwall, M. & Wouters, P. (2005). What's the deal with the Web/Blogs/the next big technology: a key role for information siceince in e-social science research? *CoLIS Lecture Notews in Computer Science, 2507*, 187–199.

Trau, R.N.C., Härtel, C.E.J. & Härtel, G.F. (2013). Reaching and hearing the invisible: organizational research on invisible stigmatized groups via web surveys. *British Journal of Management, 24*, 532–541.

Trouteaud, A.R. (2004). How you ask counts: a test of Internet-related components of response rates to a web-based survey. *Social Science Computer Review, 22*, 385–392.

Turney, L. & Pocknee, C. (2005). Virtual focus groups: new frontiers in research. *International Journal of Qualitative Methods, 4*(2), 1–10.

Vaes, J., Paladino, M.P., Castelli, L. & Leyens, J.P. (2003). On the behavioural consequences of infrahumanization: the implicit role of uniquely human emotion in intergroup relations. *Journal of Personality & Social Psychology*, 85, 1016–1034.

Van Patten, L. (2011). Rules of engagement: ten proven methods for creating and sustaining participant involvement in asynchronous online research. *QRCA Views*, Winter.

Walston, J.T., Lissitz, R.W. & Rudner, L.M. (2006). The influence of web-based questionnaire presentation variations on survey cooperation and perceptions of survey quality. *Journal of Official Statistics*, 22, 271–291.

Watson, M., Peacock, S. & Jones, D. (2006). The anlaysis of interaction in online focus groups. *International Journal of Therapy & Rehabilitation*, 13(12), 551–557.

White, M. & Dorman, S.M. (2001). Receiving social support online: implications for health education. *Health Education Research,* 16(6), 693–707.

Whitehead, L. (2011). Methodological issues in internet-mediated research: a randomized comparison of internet versus mailed questionnaires. *Journal of Medical Internet Research,* 13(4).

Williams, M. (2003). *Virtually criminal: Deviance and harm within online environments*. Unpublished doctoral dissertation, University of Wales, Cardiff: United Kingdom.

Williams, S. (2009). Understanding anorexia nervosa: an online phenomenological approach. Unpublished doctoral dissertation, United Kingdom: Queen Margaret University, Edinburgh. Retrieved from http://etheses.qmu.ac.uk/135/

Williams, S., Clausen, M.G., Robertson, A., Peacock, S. & McPherson, K. (2012). Methodological reflections on the use of asynchronous online focus groups in health research. *International Journal of Qualitative Methods*, 11(4), 368–383.

Wright, K. B. (2006). Researching internet-based populations: advantages and disadvantages of online survey research, online questionnaire authoring software packages and web survey services. *Journal of Computer Mediated-Communication*, 10(3).

Wright, K.B. & Bell, S.B. (2003). Health-related support groups on the Internet: linking empirical findings to social support and computer-mediated communication theory. *Journal of Health Psychology,* 8(1), 39–54.

Yarger, J.B., James, T.A., Ashikaga, T., Hayanga, A.J., Takyi, V., Lum, V., Kaiser, H. & Mammen, J. (2013). Characteristics in response rates for surveys administered to surgery residents. *Surgery*, 154(1), 38–45.

Yau, Y.H.C., Potenza, M.N. & White, M.A. (2013). Problematic internet use, mental health and impulse control in an online survey of adults. *Journal of Behavioral Addictions,* 2(2), 72–81.

Index

access to participants *see*
    hard-to-reach participants, 9, 10,
    55, 130–131
anonymity, 11, 16, 20–21, 55–58,
    135–136
asynchronous methods, 36–43, 64–68,
    133–143

blogs, 122–125
    benefits of blogs, 122
    preparing data for analysis, 125
    searching for blogs, 123
    sampling blogs, 125
    who people blog, 124–125

content communities, 143–147
cost, 10–11, 53–54
coverage error, 97

deception, 16–17
design issues, 98–102

email interviews, 36–43
ethical issues in online research,
    19–28, 48
    autonomy, 20–21
    confidentiality, 23–24
    copyright, 24
    debriefing, 25,154
    dignity, 20–21
    benefit and harm, 22, 27–28
    participant information page,
    150–152
    public versus private space,
    20–23
    scientific value, 21–22, 26
    social responsibility, 22, 26–27
    valid consent, 24–25
    withdrawal, 25
experiments, 112

face-to-face focus groups, 51–52
face-to-face interviews, 33–34

group online social networking *see*
    virtual communities, 143–147
guidelines for effective online
    interviewing, 45–49

hard-to-reach populations, 9, 10, 55,
    130–131
how to behave online *see* netiquette,
    28–30

incentives, 45, 61, 106
instant messaging, 43, 46–45
internet
    history and development, 1–2,
    129–130
    internet access, 4
    internet as a research tool, 2–9

microblogs, *see* twitter, 126–127
moderating, 77–78

nature of online communication,
    73–74
netiquette, 28–30
non-response error, 97–98

online data collection
    access to participants, *see* hard-to-
    reach populations, 9
    anonymity, 11, 16
    benefits of online data collection,
    9–14, 36–44, 53–59, 83–88,
    130–131
    challenges of online data collection,
    14–19, 36–44, 59–64, 88–90,
    131–133
    cost, 10–11

deception, 16–17
demand characteristics, 11
ethical issues, 19–28
flexibility & convenience, 11
hard-to-reach populations, 10, 55, 130–131
naturalistic data, 131
new social phenomena, 14
observing social behaviour, 12–13
representativeness, 14–16, 118
response rates, 17, 102–108
stigmatized identities, 13
online experiments
  attrition, 118
  demand characteristics, 117
  experimenter presence, 117
  levels of control, 118
  participant bias, 116–117
  representativeness, 118
  sample size, 113
  sample diversity and generalizability, 115–116
online focus groups
  anonymity, 55–58
  asynchronous online focus groups, 64–68
  benefits of online focus groups, 53–59
  challenges of online focus groups, 59–64
  cost, 53–54
  designing and running an online focus group, 74–79
  digital record, 59
  discussion forums see online forums, 65–67, 133–143
  drop out, 60
  duration of study, 75–76
  email distribution lists, 67–68
  group dynamics, 63–64
  hard-to-reach populations, 55
  moderating, 77–78
  non-verbal information, 60
  online environment, 76
  participant selection, 61, 75, 77
  reduction in unequal power relationships, 58–59
  size of the group, 55
  skype for focus group research, 72
  synchronous online focus groups, 68–72
  technology issues, 76–77
  timing and location, 54
  text-based chat rooms, 68
  text-based virtual reality, 68–72
  types of online focus groups, 64–72
  vocal cues, 63
  voice and video platforms, 72
online forums see virtual communities, 133–143
  amount of material, 134
  analyzing data, 138–143
  anonymity, 135
  naturally occurring conversations, 134–135
  longitudinal studies, 135
  representativeness, 135–136
  working with online forums, 136–138
online interviews
  asynchronous online interviews using email, 36–43
  data quality, 42
  guidelines for effective online interviewing, 45–49
  interview questions, 38, 48, 49
  synchronous online interviews using instant messaging, 43–45
  types of online interviews, 35–45
online surveys
  coverage error, 97
  designing your survey, 98–102
  factors affecting completion, 104–108
  host organization, 103
  incentives, 106
  invitation design, 105
  sampling error, 97
  non-response error, 97–98
  software packages, 108–110
  types of survey, 90–92
  participant information page, 150–152
  benefits of online surveys, 83–88
  challenges of online surveys, 88–90
  pre-notifications and reminders, 106
  reasons for use, 82–83

online surveys – *continued*
   response option formats, 84–86, 100
   response rates, 102–108
   sampling issues, 92–96, 104
   sources of error, 97–98
   survey length, 103
   survey topic, 103

participant information page, 150–152
phenomenological approach, 5–7

representativeness, 14, 118, 135–136
response rates, 17, 102–108

sampling
   cluster sampling, 94
   convenience sampling, 95–96
   non-probability sampling, 95
   opt-in panels, 96
   sample size in non-probability
     sampling, 96
   sampling blogs, 125
   sampling error, 97
   simple random sampling, 93
   snowball sampling, 96
   stratified sampling, 93
   systematic sampling, 93
secondlife *see* virtual second worlds,
   147–148
social media
   blogs, 122–125
   classification of social media,
     119–121

hard-to-reach populations, 130–131
history of social network sites,
   129–130
microblogs, 126–127
naturalistic data, 122–123, 131
social networking sites, 127–133
virtual communities, 133–143
content communities, 143–147
virtual second worlds, 147–148
social networking, 4, 127–133
   activity level, 4, 132
   benefits of social networking sites,
     130–131
   challenges of social networking
     sites, 131–133
   generalizing to the general
     population, 131–132
   hard-to-reach populations, 130–131
   history, 129–130
   naturalistic data, 131, 134
   validity of messages, 132–133
software packages, 78–79, 108–110,
   148–149
synchronous methods, 43–45, 68–72

translational approach, 4–5
twitter, 126–127

virtual communities, 143–147
   online forums, 133–143

youtube *see* content communities,
   143–147